Supporting physical development and physical education in the early years

Jonathan Doherty
Richard Bailey

Open University Press
Buckingham • Philadelphia

25 JAN 2005

Open University Press
Celtic Court
22 Ballmoor
Buckingham
MK18 1XW

email: enquiries@openup.co.uk
world wide web: www.openup.co.uk

and
325 Chestnut Street
Philadelphia, PA 19106, USA

First Published 2003

A catalogue record of this book is available from the British Library

ISBN   0 335 20981 5 (pb)   0 335 20982 3 (hb)

Library of Congress Cataloging-in-Publication Data
Doherty, Jonathan, 1961–
  Supporting physical development and physical education in the early years /
Jonathan Doherty and Richard Bailey.
    p. cm. – (Supporting early learning)
  Includes bibliographical references and index.
  ISBN 0-335-20982-3 – ISBN 0-335-20981-5 (pbk.)
    1. Physical education for children – Study and teaching (Early childhood)
    2. Child development.   I. Bailey, Richard, 1966– II. Title. III. Series.

GV443 .D57 2002
372.86–dc21   2002072515

Typeset by Type Study, Scarborough
Printed in Great Britain by Biddles Limited, Guildford and King's Lynn

Contents

Series editors' preface

This book is one of a series which will be of interest to all those who are concerned with the care and education of children from birth to 6 years old – childminders, teachers and other professionals in schools, those who work in playgroups, private and community nurseries and similar institutions; governors, providers and managers. We also speak to parents and carers, whose involvement is probably the most influential of all for children's learning and development.

Our focus is on improving the effectiveness of early education. Policy developments come and go, and difficult decisions are often forced on all those with responsibility for young children's well-being. We aim to help with these decisions by showing how developmental approaches to young children's education not only accord with our fundamental educational principles, but provide a positive and sound basis for learning.

Each book recognizes and demonstrates that children from birth to 6 have particular developmental learning needs, and that all those providing care and education for them would be wise to approach their work developmentally. This applies just as much to the acquisition of subject knowledge, skills and understanding, as to other educational goals such as social skills, attitudes and dispositions. In this series, there are several volumes with a subject-based focus, and the main aim is to show how that can be introduced to young children within the framework of an integrated and developmentally appropriate curriculum, without losing its integrity as an area of knowledge in its own right. We also stress the importance of providing a learning environment which is carefully planned for children's own active learning. The present volume helps us to re-think what we take so much for granted – the physical development and physical education of our young children. Perhaps it is because children, from birth, are so naturally active, that we are sometimes inclined to forget just what a significant contribution physical competence and skill can make to the emotional and social well-being of children, as well as to their general health.

Access for all children is fundamental to the provision of educational opportunity. We are concerned to emphasize anti-discriminatory approaches throughout, as well as the importance of recognizing that meeting special educational needs must be an integral purpose of curriculum development and planning. We see the role of play in learning as a central one, and one which also relates to all-round emotional, social and physical development. Play, along with other forms of active learning, is normally a natural point of access to the curriculum for each child at his or her particular stage and level of understanding. It is therefore an essential force in making for equal opportunities in learning, intrinsic as it is to all areas of development. We believe that these two aspects, play and equal opportunities, are so important that we not only highlight them in each volume in this series, but we also include separate volumes on them as well.

Throughout this series, we encourage readers to reflect on the education being offered to young children, by revisiting the developmental principles which most practitioners hold, and using them to analyse their observations of the children. In this way, readers can evaluate ideas about the most effective ways of educating young children, and develop strategies for approaching their practice in ways which exemplify their fundamental educational beliefs, and offer every child a more appropriate education.

The authors of each book in the series subscribe to the following set of principles for a developmental curriculum:

Principles for a developmental curriculum

- Each child is an individual and should be respected and treated as such.
- The early years are a period of development in their own right, and the education of young children should be seen as a specialism with its own valid criteria of appropriate practice.
- The role of the educator of young children is to engage actively with what most concerns the child, and to support learning through these preoccupations.

- The educator has a responsibility to foster positive attitudes in children to both self and others, and to counter negative messages which children may have received.
- Each child's cultural and linguistic endowment is seen as the fundamental medium of learning.
- An anti-discriminatory approach is the basis of all respect-worthy education, and is essential as a criterion for a developmentally appropriate curriculum (DAC).
- All children should be offered equal opportunities to progress and develop, and should have equal access to good quality provision. The concepts of multiculturalism and anti-racism are intrinsic to this whole educational approach.
- Partnership with parents should be given priority as the most effective means of ensuring coherence and continuity in children's experiences, and in the curriculum offered to them.
- A democratic perspective permeates education of good quality and is the basis of transactions between people.

Vicky Hurst and Jenefer Joseph

1

Moving to learn – learning to move

Action, play and movement are rich experiences in the culture of childhood.

Charlotte is 11 months old. Already she can sit up straight, reach out for interesting objects, stand up and sit down again. She can propel herself along the floor and is showing signs of desiring to walk. At first she will need some support to help her with this skill but very soon she will master it. The mobility that this offers means the world is her oyster for her to discover and move around in.

Ben has just had his third birthday. He moves quite competently around his home, walking, running and climbing stairs. He particularly enjoys riding on his new pedal toy in the park near where he lives when he goes there with his parents. They are very proud of their son's achievements and give him encouragement to help him develop his skills.

Jahneece is 5 and is in her second term in Reception class. In PE she has been learning about caterpillars and butterflies and in dance lessons she has been stretching and curling to move like these creatures. Her teacher has helped her with these movements and has been delighted with the lightness she has brought to her fluttering actions while she dances.

Introduction – movement in the lives of children

Children love to move and be physically active. They seem to derive a special, unique pleasure from running and jumping and twisting and turning, and exploring their bodies' abilities and limits. It is the contention of this book that movement experiences are of fundamental importance in each child's development and education, and that such experiences require attention and consideration by everyone who works with, teaches, helps with or brings up children.

Consider the following recent research findings (see Bailey 1999a, 1999b):

- Physical activity play is the first appearing and most frequently occurring expression of play in infants
- Children in all cultures around the world engage in both spontaneous and rule-governed forms of physical activity
- Most children would rather take part in physical activities than any other endeavour
- They would prefer to succeed in these activities than in classroom-based work
- Physical competence is a major factor influencing social acceptance in children of all ages and both sexes

- Regular physical activity can make significant positive contributions to physical, mental and emotional well-being in children.

Jerome Bruner (1983: 121) said that movement and action represent the 'culture of childhood'. In a similar fashion, Bjorkvold (1989) portrays a tension between what he terms 'child culture' and 'school culture'. This tension is outlined below:

Child culture	School culture
Play	Study
Being in	Reading about
Physical proximity	Physical distance
Testing one's own limits	Respecting boundaries set by others
The unexpected	The expected
Sensory	Intellectual
Physical movement	Physical inactivity
I move and I learn!	Sit still!

There may be very good reasons for introducing children to 'school culture' (and there may not). However, as we plan our curricula and devise our teaching methods, it is worth remembering that we are dealing with, first and foremost, children. We ignore this at our peril (and, more importantly, at their peril, too).

Movement experiences, such as physical education, playground games and informal physical activities, are among the most obvious and appealing ways of keeping in touch with 'child culture'. As such, there is a strong case for considering physical education (as broadly understood) as part of the true 'core' curriculum for young children.

A *movement education*

Numerous authors have offered their own views on the aims of physical education (PE). Talbot (1999), for example, claims that the subject 'aims to develop physical literacy and integrated development of the whole person', while Almond (2000: 12) proposes (among other things) 'moving beyond play into disciplined forms of physical activity such as sport and dance', and Parry (1998: 64) talks of 'the development of certain human excellences of a valued kind'.

In presenting the 'Case for Physical Education' at the World Summit on Physical Education, Talbot (1999: 39) lists six distinctive features of the subject which no other learning or school experience shares:

1 It is the only educational experience where the focus is on the body, physical activity and physical development;

2 It helps children to develop respect for the body – their own and others;
3 It contributes towards the integrated development of mind and body;
4 It develops understanding of the role of aerobic and anaerobic physical activity in health;
5 It positively enhances self-confidence and self-esteem;
6 It enhances social and cognitive development and academic achievement.

There are many different ways of thinking about the content and character of physical education. For this initial introduction, we are going to draw on a useful model for understanding the different elements of the physical education experience (Arnold 1979; Bailey 1999b). The model conceives physical education in terms of three general themes:

1 Education about movement
2 Education through movement
3 Education in movement.

Education about movement

This aspect stresses the value of introducing pupils to a range of physical activities, as well as the concepts, rules and procedures associated with them. Of course, there are many activities that pupils might experience, and each can make a contribution to their development and education.

The National Curriculum (Department for Education and Employment 1999c) states that all children from 5 years should experience a broad and balanced range of movement experiences, including the following:

• Dance activities
• Games activities
• Gymnastics activities.

Of course, there is no suggestion that these three types of activity represent the totality of children's movement experiences in schools. Rather, they are the minimum expected content during timetabled lessons.

In learning about movement, it is important that children come to know the range and character of the activity areas. Performance of these activities constitutes a vital aspect of this knowledge. By taking part in different structured activities, pupils can come to know how to move in particular situations to achieve certain outcomes. At the same time, they also need to come to know that some ways of moving offer success or are more aesthetically pleasing than others. An adequate physical education encompasses both kinds of knowledge: knowing how and knowing that (Bailey 1999b).

Different children enjoy and succeed in different activities, and the breadth of the physical education curriculum is a recognition of this fact. A narrow conception of a competitive team games-centred curriculum threatens to alienate a large proportion of the school population, as well as rob them of valuable learning experiences. An adequate education about movement, therefore, introduces the full range of movement experiences, and offers each pupil the opportunity to excel.

Education through movement

This aspect of the physical education curriculum refers to the use of physical activities as a means of achieving educational goals that are not necessarily part of those activities. An important aspect of this concept, and one that is particularly significant during the early years, is the contribution PE can make to work in other areas of the curriculum. Movement is particularly well placed to act as a vehicle for learning across the whole curriculum since it plays so fundamental a role in children's general learning and development.

Movement experiences can create a learning environment that is enabling and fun, which allow pupils to relax and enjoy learning. By presenting learning situations as games and play, teachers can encourage pupils who may have built up resistance to lower their defences, their frustrations and anxieties, and develop their skills and understanding incidentally as they engage in physical activity. Also, as physical activity and play are universal to all children around the world, pupils become involved in experiences that bridge differences in social or cultural background (see Bailey 1999b, for references to research in this area).

Nowhere is the potential for education through movement more apparent than in the use of language. Hopper and his colleagues (2000: 91) suggest that 'translating movements into spoken language in a variety of contexts offers a treasure chest of descriptive, directional and action words for children to explore and experience'. The scope of language usage implicit within PE is vast, and cutting across the activity areas is a language of description, quality and expression. Simply participating in PE lessons provides an environment in which pupils are led to use language naturally and purposefully. They read instructions on work-cards, record scores and devise notation systems routines, and in each case, the activity occurs in a meaningful context.

Education in movement

> If we believe in the value of education in physical activity for the . . .
> child then we believe that, by giving the child the experience (and
> skills necessary for the experience) of movement activities, we are
> introducing him/her to a 'physical' dimension which should be
> included in education for its intrinsic value and for the satisfaction
> which such movement experiences can bring.
>
> (Williams 1989: 21)

Education in movement is the most fundamental dimension of the PE
curriculum. Through engaging in physical activities and through exploring the possibilities and the limitations of those activities, pupils come to
experience them from 'inside', rather than as disinterested observers. An
important function of PE lessons must be to inspire pupils with a love of
formal and informal physical activities. To do so, teachers must realize that
PE is much more than a collection of strategies for keeping pupils fit and
healthy, or useful tricks through which to teach less palatable parts of
the curriculum. They are activities and experiences that are valuable and
worthwhile in their own right. Of course, there are powerful extrinsic
benefits to be gathered from participation in physical activities, too, but
the ultimate importance of these activities lies in their intrinsic worth.

The ultimate justification rests with the distinctive natures of physical
activity and movement, and their great importance to the lives of pupils.
Games, dance and other forms of activity represent experiences that are
valuable aspects of our culture. If pupils cannot come to see the activity
from the perspective of an 'insider', they will never recognize the true
appeal or beauty of that activity. If they are denied the opportunity of these
experiences, their education would not be complete. They are part of the
process of becoming a civilized human being (Bailey 1999b).

The content of PE

The Early Learning Goals (Department for Education and Employment
1999b) define six areas of learning for children in the Foundation Stage
(ages 3–5 years). These are personal, social and emotional development;
language and literacy; mathematical development; knowledge and understanding of the world; physical development and creative development.
The goals establish the expectations that most children will achieve by the
end of the Foundation Stage. The goal concerned with physical development seeks to support and promote 'opportunities for all children to

develop and practise their fine and gross motor skills, increase their understanding of how their bodies work and what they need to be healthy and safe' (Department for Education and Employment 1999b: 10).

In the Foundation Stage, physical development is concerned with improving children's coordination, control, manipulation and movement skills. In addition it recognizes that gains can also be expected in levels of confidence and self-esteem and in developing a positive sense of well-being.

The Early Learning Goal for physical development comprises eight statements that most children will be able to achieve by the end of the Foundation Stage. These are:

- move with confidence, imagination and in safety
- move with control and coordination
- show awareness of space, of themselves and of others
- recognise the importance of keeping healthy and those things which contribute to this
- recognise the changes that happen to their bodies when they are active
- use a range of small and large equipment
- travel around, under, over and through balancing and climbing equipment
- handle tools, construction objects and malleable materials safely and with increasing control.

> (Department for Education and Employment 1999b: 39)

The importance of Physical Education is also recognized as a foundation subject within the National Curriculum (Department for Education and Employment 1999c: 129), which states that:

> physical education develops pupils' physical competence and confidence, and their ability to use these to perform in a range of activities. It promotes physical skilfulness, physical development and a knowledge of the body in action . . . pupils discover their aptitudes, abilities and preferences, and make choices about how to get involved in life-long physical activity.

The National Curriculum for Physical Education sets out in a single attainment target the knowledge, skills and understanding that children should have achieved by the end of each of the four key stages. Four aspects provide progression both within and across the key stages, namely:

1 Acquiring and developing skills.
2 Selecting and applying skills, tactics and compositional ideas.
3 Evaluating and improving performance.
4 Knowledge and understanding of fitness and health.

During Key Stage 1 (ages 5–7 years),

> pupils build on their natural enthusiasm for movement, using it to explore and learn about their world. They start to work and play with other pupils in pairs and small groups. By watching, listening and experimenting, they develop their skills in movement and coordination, and enjoy expressing and testing themselves in a variety of situations.
>
> (Department for Employment and Education 1999c: 130)

The programmes of study at Key Stage 1 require that pupils are taught knowledge, skills and understanding through dance, games and gymnastic activities. These are the core areas of activity for the key stage and activities in these areas define the mandatory physical education experiences of children from 5 to 7 years old. Let us now consider the unique contribution each of these areas of activity has to offer.

Dance

Dance is concerned with the acquisition of control, coordination and versatility in the use of the body and assists in the maintenance and development of strength and flexibility (Department for Education and Science 1991). Through dance activities, children can explore the dynamics of movement; functional as well as expressive. Walking, skipping, galloping and stepping actions form a base for later development relating to specific step patterns and give dance its utilitarian function. Children intrinsically enjoy dance and dance activities often arise spontaneously, allowing them to explore movement in the same way as texture, colour and sound. They will respond instinctively to rhythm displaying stamps, steps, twists and jumps and move freely and confidently. Adult intervention will now help structure these natural responses into recognized dance forms.

Dance also allows children to express their reaction to each other, or the environment. Manners and Carroll (1995) believe that it is the symbolic expressive aspect of movement that gives children the opportunity to explore movement as a means of communication. It is the body that is the instrument for this expression, blending time, space, weight and flow together to capture the essential qualities of dance. In this non-verbal language children express their feelings, convey ideas and create moods when they dance. Dance has been described as 'the poetry of movement' (Department for Education and Science 1972: 45) and there is no doubt that dance has its own movement vocabulary and the interpretation of action words such as 'melt', 'plunge', 'shiver', 'explode' and 'hover' provide a perfect vent for individual expression in movement. In the same way that a writer skilfully uses words, a wide movement vocabulary is essential for a dancer to speak with skill and clarity.

Among many writers, Davies (2000) stresses the role that dance plays in children's understanding of culture and heritage. Contemporary British society reflects a richness in diversity and children's dance should include steps and forms from our folk and national dances which are integral to this country's heritage. Dance offers access to other times and cultures since dance crosses all cultures. By providing opportunities to watch performances from other countries live or on video, children will be guided to a greater understanding of multi-cultural education.

Games

Evans and Roberts (1987) report the high value children place on games, describing how children with better motor skills are likely to have better relations with peers, whilst those with less developed motor skills are disadvantaged at establishing friends. It is, however, important that the true qualities of games need to be understood by children if it is to justify its prominent position in our society. Playing games present many opportunities for learning. Wuest and Bucher (1995), for example, believe that games contribute to cognitive, psycho-motor and affective development. Many opportunities exist for communication, solving problems, teamwork, decision making, fair play and coping with winning and losing.

As Macfadyen and Osborne (2000) warn, the way children are introduced to games is important. Emphasis is on learning through fun in play-like, vigorous and challenging situations. Games in the early years comprise activities such as running, stopping and changing direction, moving in relation to others in space and hand–eye or hand–foot dexterity and coordination with equipment. Children need to practise with bats and balls of differing sizes and shapes to become competent in the skills of kicking, throwing, catching and travelling with equipment. In addition, children should be introduced to the strategies linked to playing games to improve their tactical awareness. Opportunities should exist for individual development of motor skills, cooperation leading to competition with others and a high degree of physical activity. Young children use games as part of their natural play in an all-absorbing way, developing skills and knowledge that will form the basis for later games experiences. Using games as a vehicle for lifelong learning and participation 'should be the process that will enable a child to develop a competency base that will allow him to enjoy an active and healthy adult life, both at work and at leisure' (Wetton 1988: 102).

Gymnastics

Children's natural movements as they climb, swing, roll, scramble over objects and balance are so much a part of childhood. All children enjoy the thrill of these actions, the physical challenge and the opportunity to shape their movement responses in their own creative fashion. In short, 'they do impossible things in impossible ways' (Department for Education and Science 1972: 25). A gymnastics programme aims to extend these basic skills through a series of progressive physical challenges. The focus is on the body and body management skills as children explore the range of possibilities within their own limitations of movement (Heath *et al.* 1994). By using often familiar actions, children extend their body capabilities and explore aspects of their environments as they explore the different surfaces on which they move. As they get older and increase in experience, they develop their kinaesthetic awareness and learn to judge the speed, force and directional qualities of their movements.

Gymnastics aims also to develop control and quality of movement. Movement actions comprise travelling, turning, rolling, jumping, balancing, swinging and climbing. Through work in this area, children link movements together on the floor and on simple apparatus showing understanding of concepts such as precision, body tension, stillness, extension and fluency in movements that are proficient and aesthetically pleasing. They are guided to work safely and cooperatively with other children. It is also important that they appreciate movement and can describe and talk about what they observe. Reynolds (2000) believes that gymnastics promotes problem solving, individuality and creativity; as children explore, practise and refine their actions, they are able to improve the execution of specific skills and apply this skilfulness in different contexts with imagination and ingenuity.

Swimming

Swimming is an essential survival skill, and considered so important that the Department for Education and Science (1972: 83) publication *Movement* stated that 'the ability of every individual to swim should be regarded as a civic responsibility'. According to Wetton (1988), it should be introduced to children as early as possible. She suggests that parents and other pre-school personnel play an important role in this process so that children soon become 'water happy' (p.173). Early experiences at home of moving in the bath, gurgling water and getting the face wet, and later in pre-school settings of water-trough play, filling and emptying containers, all help to build this confidence with water and the understanding of its particular properties.

Children do have a fascination with water and it provides a stimulating and fun movement experience. They delight in the immediate tactile experience of being buoyant and free from their normal body weight, discovering new orientations and the thrill of immersion and of moving through water.

Hardy (2000) divides swimming content into the three sections:

1 confidence;
2 propulsion;
3 water safety.

Confidence requires a knowledge of different aquatic environments and 'orientation', that is control of the body position in water. Propulsion involves elementary motion and the basis for efficiency in basic strokes, and water safety is empowering individuals to make reasoned judgements to keep safe in different water environments.

Although swimming and water safety activities are not statutory in Key Stage 1 of the National Curriculum, schools may choose to teach this area. The non-statutory guidelines propose that pupils should be taught to:

- move in water;
- float and move with and without swimming aids;
- feel the buoyancy and support of water and swimming aids;
- propel themselves in water using different swimming aids, arm and leg actions and basic strokes.

Outdoor play

This holds a special place in the education of young children offering experiences that assist in many areas of their development. Features in their natural surroundings are explored excitedly and can act as an added stimulus for their activities. As they react to the sights, sounds and movements of the outdoors there is often a new intensity to their physical play.

Many writers have extolled the virtues of the outdoor environment and its importance alongside the indoor environment in children's learning (see, for example, McLean 1991; Dowling 1992; Robson 1996). Lasenby (1990: 5) neatly summarizes its role, seeing it 'as an integral part of early years provision and ideally should be available to children all the time'. Research findings point to wide variation in children's outdoor play experiences. Henniger (1985) revealed that some children are inhibited socially in indoor environments and that dramatic play in boys and older children was strongly influenced by the outdoor environment. Hutt and her colleagues (1989) found boys more decisive in their choice of activities outdoors than girls, whilst Cullen (1993) found that the way boys and girls used the outdoor areas reflected gender stereotypes in play found in other studies.

Bilton (1999: 38) gives useful advice when organizing learning in the outdoors. She suggests that consideration be given to the following:

- the layout;
- the amount of space available;
- the way the environment is arranged;
- the use of fixed equipment;
- the effects of the weather;
- the need for storage.

Sutcliffe (1993) acknowledges that outdoor activity is integral to the whole learning environment but suggests that in addition it offers particular opportunities to promote physical skills and to satisfy children's sense of adventure. Outdoor physical activities have the potential to satisfy our human need for excitement and challenge in a positive way. Equipment such as climbing frames, stepping stones, playground markings, wheeled toys, trikes and bikes can assist their physical development in many ways. It encourages them to make decisions about the equipment they use in their play and they become instantly involved in solving movement problems. Additionally, they learn to trust their bodies, assess risks, cooperate with others, use various physical skills and actions in active physical involvement.

Bridging Early Learning Goals and Key Stage 1

Physical education in the early years should seek to provide a firm foundation of basic movement skills on which the next stage of children's education can successfully build (Beaumont 1997). The Early Learning Goals (ELG) provide a solid base for planning in the six areas of learning in the Foundation Stage and set out expectations for the majority of children to reach by the end of the reception class year. Planning for physical development, as in other areas should help children make progress towards and, where it is appropriate, to go beyond the goals (Department for Education and Employment 1999b).

Recommendations for planning contained within *Curriculum Guidance for the Foundation Stage* (Department for Education and Employment 1999a: 36) indicate that practitioners should give attention to:

- planning activities that offer appropriate physical challenges;
- providing sufficient space, indoors and outdoors, to set up relevant activities;

- giving sufficient time for children to use a range of equipment;
- providing resources that can be used in a variety of ways or to support specific skills;
- introducing the language of movement to children, alongside their actions;
- providing time and opportunities for children with physical disabilities or motor impairments to develop their physical skills, working as necessary with physiotherapists and occupational therapists;
- using additional adult help, if necessary, to support individuals and to encourage increased independence in physical activities.

By the time they are 5 years old, most children will have had a minimum of two terms full-time education in a Reception class and experiences in nursery or other pre-school settings. Some will be working towards the physical development ELG, whilst others will achieve beyond this during the stage. For these children achievement may be described using the level descriptions of the National Curriculum. There are eight levels (plus exceptional performance) that describe attainment in Physical Education. Children in Key Stage 1 work within Levels 1–3, with the majority of children achieving Level 2 by age 7. In applying judgements which 'best fit' children's practical performance in PE, it needs to be emphasized that these judgements should be made across the four aspects of the Pro-grammes of Study. As Maude (2001) points out, these descriptions strive to produce not only performers, but children with a broad and balanced view of PE, who can talk about what they know, are able to select and apply skills, evaluate and analyse and demonstrate understanding. The attainment target at Level 1 of the National Curriculum requires that children 'talk about how to exercise safely, and how their bodies feel during an activity', which extends the statement within the ELG for physical development, which states that most children will be able to 'recognise the changes that happen to their bodies when they are active'. Levels 2 and 3 extend this further and progress pupil attainment through the key stage.

Tables 1.1 and 1.2 illustrate how the content of PE is progressed from the Early Learning Goals through the Programmes of Study at Key Stage 1 of the National Curriculum.

Conclusion

In this chapter the significance of movement in the lives and experiences of children has been emphasized. The appeal of movement resides in its direct-ness and immediacy and can be observed in the everyday experiences of

Table 1.1 Activities to support the Physical Development Early Learning Goal

Statements	Activities
Move with confidence, imagination and in safety	• Exploring different ways of moving, e.g. running, skipping, galloping, crawling, climbing • Adjusting speed and direction to move around safely • Performing stories, action rhymes through movement • Moving to music showing pleasure and expression
Move with control and coordination	• Playing board games with dice and counters • Performing basic actions on the spot and then moving • Being able to hold a shape or remain in a fixed position • Move around safely on wheeled vehicles
Show awareness of space, themselves and of others	• Moving using fingers, hands, feet, tummies, elbows • Performing action songs with an emphasis on parts of the body • Exploring personal space. 'Pretend you are in a bubble . . .' • Playing 'Follow my leader' type games around the space
Recognize the importance of keeping healthy	• Understanding why hand washing and keeping clean is important • Knowing that exercise is important to keep the body healthy • Distinguishing between 'healthy' and 'unhealthy' foods • Recognizing the need for rest after being active
Recognize the changes to their body when active	• Do not over exert themselves physically • Recognizing that the heart beats faster after exercising • Appreciating that they may be out of breath after being active • Beginning to verbalize changes, 'My legs feel heavy!' 'I feel hot!'
Use a range of small and large equipment	• Enjoy playing on bikes, trikes and other wheeled toys • Experiencing activities with balls, bats and simple games equipment

Table 1.1   Continued

Statements	Activities
	• Exploring large indoor and outdoor climbing apparatus • Participating in parachute games with the whole class
Travel around, under, over, through equipment	• Using indoor apparatus to scramble, slide, rock and jump on/off • Using outdoor apparatus to scramble, slide, rock and jump on/off • Showing different skills on the above apparatus • Moving on and off equipment set at different heights and levels
Handle objects safely and with increasing control	Practising (un)dressing skills Using knives, forks, chopsticks, paintbrushes and crayons Playing with jigsaws, construction sets and small toys Practising skills of cutting, pasting, moulding, threading, posting

Table 1.2   Activities to support National Curriculum Physical Education (Key Stage 1)

Dance

Statements	*Activities*
Use movement imaginatively, responding to stimuli and performing basic skills	• Exploring different actions in response to stimuli, e.g. stories, poems, photographs • Copying and repeating simple stepping patterns • Utilizing leaps, twists, turns, jumps into their dances showing imagination
Change the rhythm, speed, level and direction of movements	• Varying directions – up/down/left/right/forwards/backwards • Varying speed – fast and slow • Varying level – high, medium, low
Create and perform dances, including those of different times and cultures	• Making up dances individually or with a partner • Performing hand gestures in an Indian dance with a 4-beat rhythm • Stepping patterns from traditional British folk dances, e.g. a Maypole dance
Express and communicate ideas, feelings	• Using vocabulary to describe movement, such as 'melting', 'exploding' • Talking through ways to make their dances more expressive • Responding to different styles of music, 'The music makes me happy/sad . . .'

Games

Statements	*Activities*
Travel with, send and receive a ball and other equipment	• Travelling through the teaching space with balls, hoops, skipping ropes, beanbags • Practising sending skills with such equipment to a space, a target or to a partner • Practising retrieving skills with such equipment with hands, feet, other body parts
Develop these skills for simple net, striking/fielding and invasion type games	• Improving skills of hitting a ball over a barrier to a partner (net games) • Getting better at striking a ball away from opponents (striking/fielding games) • Developing skills of sending a ball to a partner accurately (invasion games)

Table 1.2   continued

Games

Statements	Activities
Play simple, competitive games that they and others have made, using simple attacking and defending tactics	• Participating in running and chasing games • Playing games such as Dodge Ball, Keep the Basket Full, French Cricket • Devising their own games which involve awareness of attack and defence strategies

Gymnastics

Statements	Activities
Performing basic skills in travelling, being still, finding space using floor and apparatus	• Practising travelling skills on the floor to include stopping and starting • Making full use of floor space available • Performing basic skills on small apparatus
Develop their range of skills and actions	• Performing core actions such as balancing, jumping, rolling, turning • Improving skill in such core actions • Transferring basic skills onto small apparatus, e.g. benches, mats, small trestles
Choose and link skills and actions in short movement phrases	• Selecting appropriate actions from one's own movement vocabulary • Combining specific actions together from the same movement category, e.g. rolling backwards and rolling forwards • Combining specific actions together across movement categories, e.g. jumping forwards and turning
Create and perform short, linked sequences that have contrasts in direction, level and speed	• Individually making up a short movement phrase of specific actions, e.g. a roll, a jump then a balance at a low level • Individually making up a short movement phrase of specific actions, e.g. a jump, a roll to the side, then a balance • Individually making up a short movement phrase of specific actions, e.g. two fast forward rolls, a balance and a jump

young people and in the skilled performances of élite athletes. Echoing the words of Jensen that 'movement is about living and living is about learning' (2000: xii), we have argued that movement is a feature of our whole existence and a potent vehicle for all learning. Physical education, which has movement as its medium for learning, is integral to the whole education process. It is certainly the common denominator in the total development of children because of its integrating function.

Movement education is as Logsdon and colleagues have suggested 'a lifelong process of change' (1984: 12), beginning in the womb and proceeding through until the end of one's life. In the next chapter we consider physical development and show the effects of this process of change on children's movements.

2

The developing child

The development of the growing child is a complicated and dynamic process.

Every year approximately 280 million children are born throughout the world. Every year parents eagerly await the arrival of their newborn and anticipate the changes that lie ahead as their child travels the familiar path from infant to adult. Birth is the first step on this miraculous journey: it is a journey of incredible change and potential. Growth during the preceding nine months in the security of the womb has been phenomenal. The growth in the months and years ahead will be no less exciting as infancy merges into childhood.

Introduction – why is knowledge of children's physical development important?

The growing child is a dynamic individual. He or she is inquisitive, wanting to discover more about their world and use the many physical abilities they were born with. Motor skills are the special tools for exploring and expanding this environment. Through play children learn about themselves and their surroundings. Moving and growing make up much of a young child's life. It is important as parents and educators that we know as much as we can about this important aspect of development and how it fits into knowledge of the other developmental aspects, in order to be able to fully support it.

Bee (2000) tells us that physical development is a critical first step in understanding children's progress and she offers four reasons why this is so important.

1 Growth makes new behaviours possible. Specific physical changes are required for development, and a deficit in any area of physical development is likely to set a limit on what a child is capable of doing physically.
2 Growth determines experience. Children's physical capabilities have an effect on the cognitive and social development by influencing the range of experiences they have. Infants who are able to sit upright can reach for objects around them and older children who have learned to use a scooter or bike are able to investigate the wider environment more easily.
3 Growth affects others' responses. The acquisition of new skills, especially motor skills can change the way other children respond to them. Adult reactions to an infant who can crawl are different to one who cannot. For example, children who are tall and well coordinated are treated differently to children who are small or clumsy (Lerner 1985).

4 Growth affects self-concept. Physical characteristics and proficiency in physical skills significantly influences self-efficacy, or our perception of how well we achieve a particular task (Bandura 1997). The choice of activities in which to engage, social behaviour and personal sense of worth are influenced by physical experiences in early childhood.

The holistic nature of development: implications for physical education

Development is a complicated and dynamic process. Active children are products of their genetic inheritance and the environmental factors that remain throughout their development. Most complex human attributes are the result of an involved interplay between the forces of nature (heredity) and nurture (environment). Undoubtedly we are products of the 'cooperative efforts of the nature/nurture team' (Scarr and McCartney 1983: 433). Genes influence human development by affecting our experiences, which in turn influence our behaviour. From their parents, children inherit characteristics of body and mind that are the basic equipment for their journey ahead. The environment presents the conditions into which they are born and the people with whom they interact, and these will determine how they are able to use this equipment in their journey to maturity.

Physical development has a vital contribution to make to children's all-round development, since the development of movement skills influences cognitive, social and emotional development (Field 1990). Up to (and beyond) the age of 6, language and communication development is dramatic, as are other cognitive skills such as memory, attention and thinking skills. The foundations of social behaviour are laid in the early years and movement behaviour provides many of the first socializing experiences as children interact with parents and others in their environment (Nichols 1990). As children grow, their physical skills improve and the activities in which they become involved become more complex, and these factors have far-reaching implications for their development in physical education.

Many theorists have emphasized the interrelationship in the various aspects of development. Wright and Sugden (1999) stress that the resources that children bring with them, the learning that they encounter and the nature of the activity itself influence each other and in fact modify each other. Their 'transactional model' showing how the factors of development unite is presented in Figure 2.1.

In order that practitioners can maximize achievement in movement

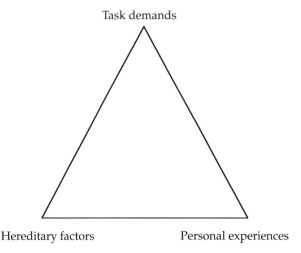

Figure 2.1   A transactional model of development.

experiences, it is important that this holistic development is acknow-
ledged. In this way we are able to interpret the different ways in which
children behave, and adapt teaching on this basis. 'This is the basis of
developmentally appropriate physical education: teaching and learning
should be planned, delivered and assessed in terms of the varied needs of
children' (Bailey 2000a: 75).

Age periods relating to development

We know that there is no such person as the 'average child'. Each child is
unique and different from all others. Yet children do have much in
common and pass through similar stages in their development. What is
important to remember, is that each has their own unique physical abilities
and sets their own pace for development.

The different stages that children pass through in developing can be
classified in a number of ways. The most common method of classifying
this is by designating periods that approximate children's chronological
age. The identified stages of development for children up to puberty
appear in Table 2.1.

Table 2.1   Stages of development in children

Age period	Age range
Prenatal	*Conception to birth*
Germinal period	Up to second week
Embryonic period	Up to 8 weeks
Foetal period	8 weeks to birth
Infancy	*Birth to 2 years*
Neonatal period	Birth to first month
Early infancy	1–12 months
Later infancy	12–24 months
Childhood	*2 to 12 years*
Early childhood	2–6 years
Later childhood	6–12 years

Prenatal development

Sarah and Mike have been together for four years and will soon be expecting their first child. They await the arrival of their baby with great excitement. During the past months they have experienced the joy of seeing Sarah's abdomen swell to provide a safe haven for the growing baby inside; they have shared the happiness of watching this baby's turns, twists and kicks and through the scan have watched this tiny being become physically much larger. As parents there are many questions in both their minds. What will the baby look like at first? What will this baby be able to do? What do we do to help our baby develop? These are the questions that surround the miracle.

Development should be viewed as a continuous process that begins at conception. Throughout the gestation period from fertilization to birth, rapid and complex physical development occurs. Even before children are born they have begun to interact with their environment. During this prenatal development, through a process of cell divisions, the single cell fertilized egg (zygote) passes through three identifiable development stages: the germinal, embryonic and foetal periods.

Let us consider this development in each of the three stages.

Germinal period

These are the first two weeks of prenatal development following conception. During the first week the fertilized egg remains almost unchanged in size and appears as a small disc 0.26 mm wide. It lives off its own yoke and receives little outside nourishment. The zygote moves down the fallopian tube and into the uterus and expands from a single cell zygote to one of about 150 cells. By this stage it has taken on the form of a fluid-filled sphere (blastocyst), which helps to protect it. The placenta, umbilical cord and amniotic sac begin to form.

Embryonic period

This is a time of huge physical changes. All of the major systems of the body, including the organs themselves, are developing. It is the stage of the greatest vulnerability to developmental defects. By the end of this period a distinct human being with arms, legs, a beating heart and a nervous system exists. By the end of the first month the embryo is approximately 6.5 mm long and grows about the same amount again each week. It takes on a more human appearance as the beginnings of the face, fingers and toes appear. Limb buds grow longer and the sex organs begin to emerge. The head is large in comparison with the rest of the body and brain development is rapid.

Foetal period

This is the longest stage and one of continuous growth. There is rapid change in both height and weight, visible sexual differentiation starts, the nervous system increases in complexity and the senses are ready to function. During the early foetal period, movement is first apparent to the mother-to-be. The foetus will respond with movement to music and voices. Research shows that the brain mechanisms responsible for musical ability are activated through influence by musical sound penetrating the uterine wall around this time (Wein 1988).

Prechtl (1986) found that movement and growth patterns are as predictable in this period as they are throughout infancy. The first reflex actions appear around the third and fourth months (De Vries *et al.* 1982). In the later foetal period there is much more activity. The cramped surroundings result in frequent changes in position, plus kicking and thrusting actions from the arms and legs. The last two months are often seen as a preparation for birth.

Development in infancy (0–2 years)

Yasmin and Imram look down adoringly at their new baby daughter Iram, born just a few hours ago. This was the small baby that Yasmin had carried within her for nine months. As she gazed at Iram she tried to recall the name she had heard for a newborn infant. Yes, that was it; neonate. Both parents had attended the prenatal classes at their local clinic and read through leaflets and information books on what to expect from a neonate. Now it was for real! What was it really like to care for a growing newborn baby? What should they, as parents, do to help her develop? How would this change as Iram got older?

Yasmin looked down and laughed. Iram was already moving and learning!

Physical development

The newborn baby was, in the past, often characterized as a helpless little being, vulnerable and ill-prepared for life outside the womb. This is far from the truth. Babies are not at all passive and are, in fact, active seekers of stimulation attending to their immediate environment in the search for stimulation. They enter the world ready to function, with all of their sensory systems working, and with an eagerness to move and learn. The child's prime task at this stage is to understand the surrounding world, and much of what the child does is centred on attempting to answer questions about this new world.

The first month of postnatal life, classed as the neonatal period, is a time of transition from the womb to the outside environment. As Krogman suggests, it is an 'adjustive time-period to being born' (1980: 9). The infant now assumes the life-giving functions that the mother had provided during the previous nine months. At birth the average newborn baby's length is about 0.5 m long and weight about 3 kg. Their head is 25 per cent of total body length and their body is 5 per cent of eventual adult size. Brain growth is rapid during these first two years. It increases from 25 per cent of eventual adult weight to 75 per cent of adult weight by the age of 2 years. Between the seventh prenatal month and the time of an infant's first birthday, the brain increases in weight by 1.7 g per day. This equates to more than 1 milligram per minute (Bee 2000).

During the first two years of an infant's life, the pace of growth is quite astounding. We see progression from a horizontal, sedentary being to a considerably larger, vertical and more active infant and this physical growth has a definite influence on motor development (Gallahue and Ozmun 1995). Height, weight, physique and maturation level all have important roles to play in the acquisition and performance of rudimentary movement patterns. Physical growth is obvious, but so are the changes that take place in the brain thus enabling the infant to acquire the dramatic skills of crawling, standing and walking. Body and mind are developing furiously! Early development lays the foundation for the young child's physical abilities and in the performance of skilled motor actions. By 2 years of age most children can walk, talk and are eager to explore their environments. Their thirst for more knowledge is insatiable. In this period they are gradually acquiring greater mastery over their bodies; movements are becoming more skilful and these replace the less coordinated actions of babies.

Alongside rapid increases in height and weight during the first two years, changes also occur in body proportions. These reflect the principles of both *cephalocaudal* and *proximodistal* development. Cephalocaudal development is that which proceeds longitudinally from the head towards the feet. When born, the neonate has an appearance of being 'all head'. This is not far from the truth, as it is almost 70 per cent of the eventual adult size, representing 25 per cent of its total body length. At 1 year old, the head accounts for 20 per cent of body length. By adulthood, the head accounts for 12 per cent and the legs 50 per cent of total stature (Shaffer 1999). Proximodistal development is growth proceeding from the centre of the body to the periphery. In prenatal development, the chest and internal organs form first, followed by arms and legs, and finally hands and feet. These trends in development are easily observable in infants and children as they show greater coordination in their upper bodies than in legs and feet. When beginning to write and draw, gross shoulder movements are seen long before fine motor forms are developed (Gabbard 1992).

Perceptual-motor development

In the first year, an infant's visual system matures rapidly. Less than a year ago as babies, only able to see highly contrasting patterns or objects that move (Banks and Ginsburg 1985), infants are capable of making increasingly complex visual discriminations and organizing what is seen to perceive visual forms (Shaffer 1999). The eyes grow rapidly during the first two years. Visual acuity, which refers to the amount of detail that can be seen, develops quickly. As a newborn the length of focus is between 10 and 25 cm and approaches normal adult acuity within a year (Aslin and Dumais 1980). Peripheral vision, which refers to the visual field observed with no change in the fixed position of the eyes, improves rapidly, so that by 5 months vision is 40 degrees from the centre (Aslin and Salapatek 1975). Adult peripheral vision is about 90 degrees on either side. Tracking is the ability to direct the eyes from one line of sight to another. Research by Aslin (1981) found evidence of tracking in infants as young as 6 weeks. Depth perception, which is the ability to judge how far away an object is from oneself, first appears between 2 and 6 months (Svejda and Schmidt 1979); and form perception, that is the ability to distinguish between different shapes, at a similar age (Cohen *et al*. 1996).

The development of auditory (hearing), olfactory (smell) and tactile-kinesthetic (touch) perception, reflects a similar steady development in the first two years.

Early infant movement

Newborn babies bring with them a wealth of abilities that enable them, not only to survive, but to interact with the world and engage in a much wider range of activities than was perhaps previously believed (Brazelton 1984). Any account of infant development must consider the important role that reflexes play. Most early movement is characterized by reflex actions. Cratty defined these as 'involuntary actions triggered by various kinds of external stimuli' (1979: 49). These are the earliest movements elicited in the newborn infant. Shaffer (1999) informs us that early reflexes can be categorized into two groups:

Survival reflexes
These have a clear adaptive value. Examples here include the eye-blink reflex (which protects against strong light or foreign bodies entering it), sucking and swallowing reflexes for food intake. The rooting reflex also assists in feeding as the child touched on its cheek will turn in the direction to suck.

Primitive reflexes
These are the precursors of voluntary movement. They indicate how deeply movement activities are linked to the nervous system. The grasping reflex may help infants carried on their mothers' hips to hold on, the stepping reflex may pave the way for later walking and running and the swimming reflex would keep an infant afloat if accidentally immersed in water (see Table 2.2).

Reflex movements are the basis for later voluntary movements (Bower 1976; Thelen 1980) and are normally phased out after the first few months of life. The reason is that as the higher centres of the cortex area of the brain

Table 2.2 Primitive reflexes in infants

Reflex	Triggering stimulation	Response
Babinski	Stroke the sole of the foot	Spreads toes, foot in
Grasping	Caress the palm of the hand	Makes a fist
Startle	Awareness of a sudden noise	Head back, limbs extend
Rooting	Stroke the cheek	Head turns, mouth sucks
Swimming	Submerge in water	Swimming actions
Walking	Simulate walking action	Legs show stepping actions

mature, they begin to guide voluntary movement actions and take over from the lower subcortical areas that originally controlled them. In this way they assume control over elementary movements such as walking, swimming, climbing and so on. Although cortical control becomes dominant, the function of the subcortex is never completely inhibited and can be seen in controlling coughing, sneezing or yawning actions throughout one's life. There is some debate over the exact cause of this but there is general agreement that there is at least an indirect link between early reflexive behaviour and later voluntary movements in children (Gallahue and Ozmun 1995).

Movement in neonates is not limited to reflexive behaviour. In contrast, spontaneous movements appear in the absence of any stimuli (Thelen 1979; Hofsten and Ronnqvist 1993). These movements do not appear to be goal-oriented and infants appear to be absorbed in kicking, waving and rocking actions for the sake of the activity. In a study by Clark (1988), seven common types of movement were identified. They were (1) alternate leg kicking, (2) single leg kicking, (3) kicking with both legs together, (4) arm waving, (5) rocking, (6) arm banging against a surface and (7) finger flexing.

Other movements have been observed, which are not of a reflex nature either. After feeding, for example, infants exhibit slow movements that alternate limb flexion and extension. When asleep, they exhibit frowns, sucking movements and also rapid eye movement (REM). On awakening, there are isolated but progressive body movements that later become continuous. Movement of the fingers and toes are also common. Such movements are not related to gender, but to state of arousal, positioning and temperature factors. Supine infants exhibit more stretch movements and head turns than in prone positions. Babies are more active when on their backs than lying face down. Korner and colleagues (1985) found that the most active neonates grew into children with high daytime activity patterns and parents reported these same infants as more likely to approach new experiences with confidence as young children.

There is still debate about these types of early movement. They do appear to have no particular purpose or goal, but their appearance is quite predictable and ordered. Although appearing spontaneous, researchers have identified organizing constraints for the movements, with an underlying structure evident. This adds credence to the dynamical properties of the human body (Gabbard 1992).

The period from 12 to 24 months is a time for the infant to practise and master many of the movement actions initiated during the first year and add new ones. The idea of the helpless baby lying inert for long periods at a time without the need for mental or physical stimulation is incorrect. As we have seen already, babies do not stay still for long. They demand stimulation in the environment around them; and they want to move! Although the rate of acquisition of skills varies according to each individual, the sequence of skills is predetermined by innate biological factors that transcend social, cultural and ethnic boundaries (Gallahue and Ozmun, 1995). Findings from research during the 1930s and 1940s established the creation of 'motor milestones' (Gesell 1939). These are basic to skilled performance as each skill is a landmark in an individual's motor development.

In the first two years, the immediate environment around the child presents three categories of movement to be mastered:

1 stability,
2 locomotion,
3 manipulation.

Stability

This refers to the relationship of the body to gravity whilst maintaining an upright posture. Gabbard (1992) states that the ability to achieve postural control of the body and move it voluntarily to a desired position underlies all motor behaviour. Stability is therefore central to all categories of movement because it is involved to some degree in all voluntary movement.

Locomotion

This is the capacity to move around one's environment. Having gained control over gravity and remaining upright alone, the infant is now ready to proceed with walking, perhaps the most important landmark in motor development (Gabbard 1992). Before this complex feat is achieved, however, the infant will attempt a number of ways of moving around its environment, namely crawling and creeping actions. Although walking is in evidence in some children by 9 months, most infants by 13 months will have achieved the monumental milestone of walking independently. This is significant because no longer is the infant a spectator, but is now able to move around and explore the environment independently (Haywood 1993).

Manipulation

This area of motor development is characterized by three terms. First, prehension, which describes initial voluntary use of the hands and includes actions such as seizing and grasping. Second, manipulation refers to skilful use of the hands, seen in activities such as painting or stringing beads and occurs in later childhood (ages 5–8 years). Third, manual control encompasses both aspects together.

By 8 months many infants can receive two objects together and by 9 months will be able to operate a pincer grip. This changes a somewhat inaccurate fumbler into a skilled manipulator of knobs and dials who enjoys using his newly acquired hand skills. By 16 months, manipulation has become coordinated and proficient.

In spite of the ability to combine simple motor activities into more complex sequences, the skills of 2-year-olds are not sufficiently developed to allow them to catch a ball easily or to use the new skills of cutting or colouring accurately. These, and others, become the skills for early childhood. A summary of the main movement skills in the first two years of a child's life are shown in Table 2.3, whilst a more detailed account is given in Table 2.4.

Table 2.3 Ages at which movement skills are achieved

Age range (months)	Milestone
0.7–4.0	Head held erect
0.7–5.0	Turns from side to back
1.0–5.0	Sits upright with support
4.0–8.0	Unilateral reaching
5.0–9.0	Sits alone unsupported
5.0–12.0	Pulls up to stand position
7.0–12.0	Walks with assistance
9.0–16.0	Stands alone
9.0–17.0	Walks alone

(*Source*: Haywood 1993)

Table 2.4 Supporting movement experiences in infancy

Age	Physical development		Perceptual-motor development
	Gross motor activities	Fine motor activities	Integrated activities
0–6 months	• Physical contact, much lifting and carrying • Massage body and limbs after bathing • Lying supine, kick with no nappy on • Lying on tummy playing with toys • Pull up from lying on back using hands. Pushing soles of feet against your palms	• Smile, give opportunity to respond • Repeated gripping of your index finger • Place a small object in their palm to hold • Place objects above cot outside their reach • Prepare for their feed within reach range • Let them play with a rattle	• Pick them up, talk face to face with them • Provide bright, stimulating environment • Introduce to different everyday sounds • Put bright, moving mobiles above the cot • Hang rattles and toys over the pram • Place coloured objects within their vision
6–12 months	• Place toys around the room in their sight • Encourage exploration of environment • Assist to stand up regularly • Allow time in a baby walker • Use a playpen as a support frame • Increase space between room furniture	• Place toys around them where they sit • Let them play with stacking beakers • Let them explore objects with both hands • Play with a rolling ball when sitting up • Encourage a pincer grip when picking up • Use action rhymes with hand moves	• Give them a play mat of different textures • Have toys which make a noise on touch • Change sitting position to observe more • Place toys in full view in easy reach • Let them visually track a moving toy • Move toys in different directions to track

Table 2.4 Continued

Age	Physical development		Perceptual-motor development
	Gross motor activities	Fine motor activities	Integrated activities
12–18 months	• Provide wheeled push-and-pull toys • Let them use large sit-and-ride toys • Practise kicking a ball • Get them to pick up toys from the floor • Mirror balancing activities • Supervise but encourage stair climbing	• Encourage tower building with bricks • Set up activities for water play • Let them experiment with play dough • Encourage play with shape sorters • Provide stacking beakers • Introduce inset-board puzzles	• Play hide-and-seek games with playthings • Play pointing games with familiar objects • Try simple visual memory games • Set up simple movement challenges • Play naming of body part games • Use activities with longer concentration
18–24 months	• Provide balls to roll and throw • Use whole body action rhymes • Extend use of large wheeled toys • Let them explore large open spaces • Move around on playground equipment • Encourage dancing to taped music	• Put together a treasure chest of small toys • Let them thread beads on string • Provide jigsaws of different sized pieces • Encourage using hand puppets • Make finger paints and crayons available • Have hammer-and-peg activities ready	• Provide un-tuned musical instruments • Give them colouring books to use • Encourage strategies to solve problems • Let them play matching and sorting games • Replace toys correctly after play • Arrange to play with other children

Development in early childhood (2–6 years)

Mark and Jenni are 4-year-old twins. They attend a local nursery because their mother Karen felt that they both need the company of other children and the stimulation that such an environment offered. Both engage in non-stop physical activities from the time they wake up in the morning until bedtime. The afternoon naps are now gone for both children and their days are filled with exploring their world and using existing physical skills better, and learning new ones. They enjoy the opportunities for movement that the nursery can offer and already Jenni has shown a liking for climbing apparatus delighting herself and others through her skills.

The years from 2 to 6 are a time of rapid change for young children. Inquis-itive and full of energy, they are keen to discover more about their world and the things they can do in it. Their quest is supported by a marked increase in their physical capacities, memory and thinking skills. They become influenced by members of their family and peers as they begin to develop social skills in their play. It is an exciting time for them, full of activity as they test the limits of their developing skills. Indoors they are seen building with bricks, painting, cutting and doing puzzles, whilst out-doors much of their time is spent running, climbing and chasing. Let us now take a closer look at this developing physical prowess.

Physical development

The most striking difference between the infant and the young child is one of proportion. In this stage, growth is not as rapid as in infancy. What has changed is appearance. Pre-school children take on a different silhouette to that of infants. They appear taller and leaner and their heads do not look disproportionately large for their bodies. This is on account of greater growth in leg length than in trunk and head size.

By age 4, the child has doubled the birth length but gain in weight is less than the amount gained in the first year of life (Gallahue and Ozmun 1995). Gender differences here are minimal. An increase in bone density means the child is much more able to manipulate his body, which in turn increases independence in his movement activities. Girls at birth have more fat tissue than boys and this difference is a little more evident in the childhood years. Maturation in muscle tissue occurs steadily during child-hood, with accompanying increases in muscle mass and strength for both boys and girls.

There are at the same time neurological changes. By age 3, the brain is 90 per cent adult size and by 5 it is almost full size (Tanner 1978). By age 5, children have developed a dominant cerebral hemisphere (usually the left side), which is responsible for speech and language functions. In childhood there begins to be a reliance on one hemisphere or another to serve particular purposes. In an experiment where children were asked to pick up a crayon, kick a ball, look into a small bottle and listen to a sound, 32 per cent of children in this age phase showed a consistent lateral preference by relying on one side of the body exclusively (Coren *et al.* 1981). Handedness, the preference for using one foot or one hand, is well established in children of 6 years. The process of myelination, which allows the transmission of nerve impulses, continues and is complete by the end of early childhood. Following myelination, movement patterns can increase in complexity and this accounts for the levels of mastery in motor skills characteristic of this period.

Perceptual-motor development

Sensory apparatus continue to develop in this period. Visual acuity steadily increases until the age of 5 when adult levels are attained (Lowrey 1986). The component of dynamic visual acuity that allows the direction and speed of an object to be monitored is notably improved during this period (Williams 1983), which leads to improvements in throwing and catching ability. According to Gabbard (1992), spatial orientation develops steadily and reports that by 4 years old, most children are aware of basic dualisms such as over/under, high/low, top/bottom and vertical/horizontal.

Other visual processes develop accordingly also. The ability to distinguish an object from its background (called figure–ground perception), which is useful in catching activities, improves between the ages of 4 and 8. Depth perception, used when replacing a top on a bottle or judging the distance to throw a ball in a rounders game is refined up until the age of 12 years. Visual-motor behaviours, common in the childhood period, such as stacking cubes, stringing beads, drawing lines with more control and using utensils, continue to develop during the childhood period.

Kinesthetic acuity, or the ability of the body to detect differences in location, distance, force or speed of the body approaches adult levels by age 8. Research has shown that kinesthetic memory, or the ability to reproduce movements from memory, decreases in errors in performance after the age of 5 (Keogh and Sugden 1985). By 5 years children have sufficient body awareness to accurately identify major body parts and by 6 or 7 have the ability to distinguish minor parts such as wrists, elbows and ankles

(Williams 1983). Directional awareness is the internal awareness of the different sides of one's body and an ability to identify dimensions in external space. By age 3 many children will be able to place an object correctly in front or behind their bodies, but will experience difficulty in putting objects in front or behind another one. A year later, most will be able to position objects 'to the side' (Gabbard 1992).

The ability to balance is considered an important component in motor development (Ulrich and Ulrich 1985). Findings report improvement with age but point to superior performances on static balances in girls (Malina and Bouchard 1991). Perceptual integration, which is the translation of information from one sense to another, although partly functional at birth, improves with age beyond the childhood years. Such functioning is common in motor skill situations, where the skill requires the interaction of visual, tactile or kinaesthetic information. Stop to watch a youngster hopping and clapping in time to music and you will realize that this integration is not fully developed in early life. Improvements in all these systems are observable and increase steadily throughout the period of childhood (Williams 1983).

Movement development

Between the ages of 2 and 7 years, the movement capabilities of children enter a period of acceleration. This is the time when 'children lay the foundations for a lifetime of movement' (Bailey 2000a: 78). It is a time for developing mastery in generic movement skills and for children to test themselves physically in different environments. Children of this age enjoy the thrill of discovering how fast they can run, how quickly they can climb, if they can travel across the monkey bars and master the slide in the playground or park.

Movement activities can be viewed from various perspectives but all are based around the three categories described earlier; namely stability, locomotion and manipulation as these are found in the movement behaviours for all ages. One common classification is into fine motor and gross motor activities (Malina and Bouchard 1991). Fine motor activities involve movements that require precision and dexterity, usually regulating the use of hands and eyes together. Movement patterns in this category range from writing, drawing, cutting, pasting and the manipulation of small objects and instruments. Gross motor activities involve the whole body or major segments. Often referred to as 'fundamental motor skills', they include such skills as running, jumping, galloping, hopping, throwing and kicking (Williams 1983). There is some overlap between these categories as certain activities involve both. For example throwing a frisbee to a partner requires speed and power to project it (gross) and accuracy to aim it correctly (fine).

Fine motor development

Whereas infants use their hands to point with, wave, grasp and release, changes occurring during early childhood allow increased control in many finger movements (Carlson and Cunningham 1990). As a result, young children's control in holding pencils, placing pegs in pegboards and stringing beads becomes more precise. Progress in a child's ability to copy or draw designs begins at about 1 year with scribbling. A typical 3-year-old is able to draw good horizontal lines and circles and add to this squares and triangles over the next two years (Knobloch and Pasamanick 1974). More detailed artwork now becomes possible. By age 5 there is a definite organization in relationship to the visual model but copying will continue to be refined up to age 9 (Ayres 1978). Birch and Lefford (1967) found that children's tracing abilities are at a mature stage by age 6.

Forming letters presents many children with a challenge. Many children of age 4 can print recognizable letters and with practice children of 5 are able to print their first name. By age 6 many can print the alphabet and numbers up to 10. As control improves the height of letters and numbers decreases, but the ability to space them is not refined until about age 9 years (Gabbard 1992).

Aspects of dressing prove difficult for the average 3-year-old who struggles to pull on and off socks, wrap a scarf or fasten buttons. By 5 most children can accomplish these tasks of finger dexterity and manipulation. Fastening a zip in a coat or tying shoe-laces are challenges to the preschool child, but many 5-year-olds are proficient here too. Such increase in fine motor control brings with it certain independence, which corresponds with these children's desire to help themselves.

Gross motor development

There is a wealth of research concerning the development of the fundamental motor skills of childhood (Wickstrom 1983; Cratty 1986; Gallahue 1989). The following section describes some of the important gross motor skills and their development through early childhood. Stability abilities, according to Gallahue (1993) comprise axial movements and postures. Axial movements refer to trunk or limb movements that orient the body while stationary. These actions are seen in twisting, bending, stretching and swinging movements in gymnastics and dance. Postures involve supporting the body, rolling, dodging, as well as static and dynamic postures. Performing a cartwheel is an example of a dynamic balance showing postural stability.

Locomotor actions embrace a range of gross motor skills. Running is seen between the ages of 2 and 3 but lacks the ability to stop and start efficiently. By age 5 there are observable improvements in form and in speed and this increases from 5 to 8 years. There are no significant differences in average running speed between the sexes at this time (Malina and Bouchard 1991). Jumping is considered a more difficult skill to master due to the strength required for taking off and the postural control required for landing. The leap, which is a jump off from one foot to land on the other is achieved by age 2 but maximum height and distance accomplished at age 4 or 5 (Gabbard 1992). Climbing is a skill that pre-school children are keen to master. Early climbing is seen in 'marked-time climbing', where one foot is brought up to meet the other before the next step is taken (Schickedanz et al. 1993). Other locomotor actions of galloping, sliding and skipping combine basic movements and because of their complexity are not mastered until the end of the early childhood years.

Gallahue and Ozmun (1995) propose that manipulative movements are generally combined with other movement forms. The propulsive skill of striking occurs commonly with stepping, swinging or turning movements and receptive movements such as trapping may involve bending or stepping also. Rolling a ball precedes catching it. By the end of the early childhood period, children will place their feet in anticipation of receiving the ball and track it at different heights and speeds through the air. Throwing efficiency develops in early childhood to incorporate a shift in weight and later a step with the foot opposite the arm throwing (Cratty 1979). Younger children throw solely with their arm, whereas older children coordinate more muscle groups and so are able to throw further. Apart from strength differences, older children use a more refined technique of movement (Gallahue 1989).

Table 2.5 gives a summary of these refined movement skills and more detailed information is found in Table 2.6.

Psycho-social factors affecting children's movement development

The years from birth to 6 are important in the emergence and advancement of social skills in children and physical education offers a powerful vehicle to enable this to happen. From birth, infants attempt to make sense of the social and emotional context that surrounds them as they begin to shape their relationships with other people. They also learn appropriate social

Table 2.5 Movement skills in early childhood

Age	Fine skills	Gross skills
3 years	Picks up blocks Places shapes in holes Turns pages of a book Paints at an easel	Stands on one foot Walks backwards and sideways Jumps down from a step Kicks a large ball with force
4 years	Holds pencil in adult way Copies a square accurately Brings thumbs into opposition Colours inside lines	Pedals a tricycle Hops on the spot and along Bounces a large ball Runs smoothly
5 years	Uses a knife and fork competently Threads a needle and sews Copies a triangle accurately Does jigsaws with joining pieces	Can touch toes when upright Jumps for height up to 30 cm Dances rhythmically to music Walks downstairs with alternating feet
6 years	Ties own shoelaces Writes first and last names Holds a pencil with fingertips Builds straight towers of cubes	Skips with alternate feet Catches a ball with consistency Kicks a football up to 6 metres Throws a ball using wrists and fingers

behaviour. They learn by observing others who act as role models – parents, carers, teachers and their peers – and internalize those observed behaviours (Bandura 1969). Social learning is an extremely powerful influence on children's holistic development. Physical educators have long held that social development of children is an important goal of the whole physical education experience. For many, social development has been seen as an automatic result of any group experiences in PE. For this claim to have credence, it is important that social objectives within this area are clearly articulated. This requires that programmes designed to meet social objectives can be planned and evaluated to gauge the extent to which success here has been achieved. It also guards against activities that are not planned carefully with regard to social development that could have a detrimental effect on lifelong motor development.

According to Nichols (1990), social objectives in physical education focus their emphasis in two directions. First, the experiences should contribute to the development of skills important for life in a democratic society. The importance of teaching children social values in educating young people to

Table 2.6 Supporting physical activity in early childhood

Age	Physical development		Perceptual-motor development
	Gross motor activities	*Fine motor activities*	*Integrated activities*
2 years	Let child run freely avoiding obstacles Provide opportunities to climb outside Encourage direction in wheeled toy play Introduce to small tricycles Promote walking up/down stairs alone	Let child scribble in circles, lines and dots Encourage turning pages in picture books Develop grip on a pencil Challenge child to build a tower of 7+ cubes with both hands	Encourage play with construction toys Encourage confidence in drinking from beakers Assist with everyday household tasks Become involved in musical games
3 years	Set up simple obstacle courses for wheeled vehicles Give time to practise riding a tricycle Develop throwing and kicking actions Allow active pretend play with peers	Let child copy building patterns with cubes Let child cut out designs with scissors Help child to eat using a knife and fork Give assistance with fastening buttons Direct how to dry hands after washing	Let them help in making and using percussive and shaking instruments Involve them in cookery activities Monitor spatial skills when manoeuvring in obstacle courses
4 years	Join in running, hopping games Let child practise steering on a tricycle Help to refine throwing for accuracy skill Provide safe balancing challenges Encourage use of climbing frames	Provide different art and craft materials to help drawing and modelling skills Continue assisting with dressing skills Continue sand and water play Help develop simple computer skills	Play lotto and other matching games Give instructions for physical tasks in different voices – slow/fast/whisper, etc. Ask them to verbalize how they solved a physical problem

Table 2.6 Continued

Age	Physical development		Perceptual-motor development
	Gross motor activities	Fine motor activities	Integrated activities
5 years	Seek to develop agility in locomotor skills alone and with peers Maintain variety in large play equipment Allow ample opportunities for climbing, swinging and sliding out of doors	Seek development of control over pencils and paintbrushes Provide more elaborate construction kits Refine mouse and typing skills in computing	Increase the complexity of matching tasks using shapes and colours Help with aiming skills using balls Let them make up their own games with friends
6 years	Introduce a two-wheeled bicycle using stabilizers Encourage playground skipping games Let child practise skills taught in school at home Praise development	Extend cookery skills Help to sustain good writing technique in stories, lists, recipes, letters, etc. Assist skill development in throwing and catching through fun games	Introduce a new physical activity Promote opportunities for vigorous exercise outside school Target skill development in an area of weakness

be responsible and participatory members of our society is recognized, too, in the professional literature (Department for Education and Employment 1999c). Being part of a democracy requires each individual to assume certain responsibilities both for themselves and for their actions, and to possess adequate social skills to interact with others. Physical education experiences offer particular environments that foster the learning of social skills. Specifically, these skills comprise, among others, working alone and alongside others, accepting individual differences, sharing in decision making and assuming different roles within a team.

The second direction involves fostering social skills for participation in physical activities. These are relevant not only to a particular age group, but also in the development of lifelong physical activity. Skills here include cooperating with others, learning how to compete, playing fairly and accepting losing. In PE, social skills occur in many different social environments, with each setting dictating its expected values and norms for behaviour.

Using the social objectives identified by Nichols (1990), Table 2.7 gives examples relevant to various PE settings.

Table 2.7 The relationship between social objectives and physical education contexts

Social objectives	Physical education context
Controlling one's behaviour	Not becoming frustrated at not being able to catch a thrown ball
Working alone and with others	Developing sending and receiving skills with a large ball
Taking turns	Waiting for a free space on the climbing frame
Respecting equipment	Returning games equipment to the correct basket after use
Following rules and instructions	Listening to the teacher's instructions in the swimming pool
Sharing ideas. Sharing decision making	Making up a partner dance to a simple musical stimulus
Taking responsibility for one's actions	Understanding that barging into others in the playground is not acceptable
Playing fairly	Respecting the rules of the game and adhering to them
Being a good winner. Accepting losing	Not boasting to others about being the fastest runner in the class
Accepting responsibility for various roles	Being a group leader in a simple orientation activity outdoors

Conclusion

The period from birth to 6 years is one of huge changes in the growth and development of the child. Physical changes in height and weight make it a crucial time for developing motor skills. Perceptual mechanisms, too, which include the ability to use sensory information about the environment and make movement decisions are improving rapidly. An increase in body awareness allows children to adapt their skills to new movement situations and as a result of development in the neuromuscular systems, we can see a refinement in a host of movement tasks. Intellectual development brings with it a deepening understanding of the potential for movement and socially the children become more aware of others in their environment and learn to interact with them in different settings.

The implications for physical education are huge. For those involved in planning physical experiences for young children, the central role of the whole child needs to be borne in mind. Learning experiences should be planned which account for individual differences in development and which meet the needs of each child. It is only if the overall needs of all children are met that we can say that physical education experiences have been successful.

3

Movement learning

The ability to perform a variety of physical skills is at the heart of human existence.

Annika is 3 and can often be seen sitting on the carpet in the playgroup with a set of building bricks. She particularly enjoys stacking them to build towers. Often as many as eight bricks are placed carefully on top of each other to build a straight tower. What process has she gone through to enable her to perform this skill?

Ben, aged 5 loves to play on the climbing frame in his local park. He can scramble up the netting and swing on the rope at the top. He has learned how to coordinate his arm actions so he can go the whole way across the monkey bars without stopping. Afterwards he likes to slide down the pole like a fireman. How has he learned these skills? How can he improve his skills?

Introduction – understanding movement learning

Taking a holistic view of child development, it is not surprising that the range of factors associated with physical development is diverse – biological, motor, perceptual and social. Although there is no single frame of reference to encompass all aspects of development, there is a distinct advantage in adopting a single perspective. Motor learning and development in the past have been viewed from many different perspectives and each one contributes to the expansion of our knowledge. Historically, influential approaches have been the 'maturation approach' (Gesell 1939); 'normative approach' (Espanshade 1947); and the 'cognitive approach' (Piaget 1952).

More recently two approaches have emerged: the 'information processing approach' (Siegler 1996; Klahr and MacWhinney 1998) and the 'dynamic systems approach' (Thelen et al. 1989; Thelen 1995). In relation to how children acquire physical skills, these latter two approaches are now described in more detail.

Information –processing approach

Emerging in the early 1970s the information-processing approach became the dominant perspective for physical educationalists interested in motor learning. Theorists are concerned how the individual uses information to perceive, make decisions and organize actions in relation to the demands placed on him by the environment. Schmidt (1988) has conceptualized the approach in terms of a simple analogy between the mind and a computer (see Figure 3.1).

The human mind receives information from the environment through

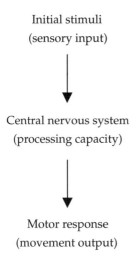

Initial stimuli
(sensory input)

Central nervous system
(processing capacity)

Motor response
(movement output)

Figure 3.1 A simplified version of the information-processing model.

the senses, processes it and outputs it as movement. Schmidt's schema theory highlights three separate stages through which information must pass from input to output. In the stimulus-identification stage (1) the system decides the nature of the presented stimulus. If the task was to throw a beanbag into a hoop on the ground, the system at this stage would identify the specific movement patterns involved, whether the stimulus was moving or stationary and its location to the thrower. This analysis is achieved through the relevant senses, predominately vision, touch and kinesthesis and the total information is assembled ready to be passed onto the next stage.

The task of the response-programming stage (2) is to decide what movement to make from the individual's repertoire of movements. In relation to the aiming task above, this stage would choose the best type of grip, stance and throw for the occasion based on knowledge of the environment and the child's personal movement experiences. The final response-programming stage (3) organizes the motor system for the movement selected. Lower level mechanisms in the brain stem and spinal cord are made ready and a motor programme that will control the movement is prepared. This programme directs the appropriate muscles to contract in the proper sequence, with accompanying levels of force and timing to produce the final movement.

Also underlying skilled performance are the characteristics of attention, memory, processing speed and programming strategies that are associated with the ability to process information in this model. These developmental characteristics will be discussed later in the chapter.

Dynamic systems approach

This approach seeks to answer questions of process in motor behaviour. Many traditional approaches have concentrated on the ordered emergence of skills linked to the development of the central nervous system (e.g. grasping, creeping, walking, etc.), but have not addressed the ' why' questions that result in these observable movement actions. The dynamic systems approach emphasizes the importance of the dynamic and self-organizing properties of the motor system and proposes that the control of movement action is as a result of the dynamical properties of muscle collectives. The control of any movement is a result of several systems working together in a dynamic and cooperative manner. No one system takes preference as all the systems interact in a way that is independent of any one subsystem. Movement patterns produced are the result of an interaction of these systems and are in response to unique factors within the task, the environment and the individual. Enquiry in the dynamic systems approach has already illuminated many areas in the learning of children's motor skills, for example in stepping patterns (Thelen and Ulrich 1991), reaching (Thelen *et al.* 1993) and independent walking (Clark and Phillips 1993).

The individuality of the learner is fundamental in this theory, postulating that each person has their own unique timetable or ' biological clock'. Although, as we have seen, motor skills occur sequentially, the rate of development and the extent is determined individually and influenced by the task itself and factors in the environment. Basic motor skills do not simply unfold as part of a 'master plan', rather they are learned because goal-driven infants continually recombine their actions into new and more complex ones that help them achieve their movement goals. The skills described in the previous chapter represent an active reorganization of existing capabilities undertaken by the curious active infant with a particular goal or objective in mind.

Learning factors influencing motor skill acquisition

For the past few weeks Lauren and her friend Jo (both aged 6) have desperately wanted to learn to skip. Their parents have supported this and bought each girl a new rope. For the past few weeks they have observed other children demonstrating their skills at rope jumping and as a result, every day at break time and during lunch they find a quiet corner of the playground and with their ropes can be seen bobbing up and down. With each day of practice, both girls have improved their techniques considerably. Lauren has a good rhythm and wants to develop her speed skipping while Jo is already trying out some tricks that she has seen her elder sister Lynne performing.

How can Lauren learn to skip faster? Will Jo be able to learn new rope skills? What are the factors that influence the learning of physical skills?

'Learning' is a relatively permanent change in behaviour as a result of practice or experience and 'performance' is a function of learning and other variables (Nichols 1990). The two terms are clearly not synonymous. The responsibility for those who plan and teach physical education to young children is to provide experiences for the growing, moving and thinking young person which will assist in acquisition and development of a range of motor skills. Factors for consideration are given in Table 3.1 and will be returned to in more detail later.

The ability to perform a variety of physical skills is at the heart of human existence and, not surprising there exists many interpretations of the term 'skill'. Most interpretations concur in the main with Guthrie's (1952: 136) classic definition of the term as, 'the ability to bring about some end result with maximum certainty and minimum outlay of energy, or of time and energy'. Such a definition emphasizes four key elements:

1 It implies action directed towards a specific objective, such as holding a headstand in gymnastics.
2 It involves the achievement of an end result with certainty, rather than relying on chance or luck.

Table 3.1 Factors affecting the learning of physical skills

Physical environment	Motor learning variables	Personal characteristics
Facilities	Practice opportunities	Age
Equipment	Learning styles	Gender
Location	Reinforcement	Maturation
Weather	Transfer	Motivation
Safety	Retention	Abilities
Temperature	Feedback	Temperament
Clothing	Instruction	Previous experiences

3 Energy in the production is conserved, resulting in economic and efficient movements.

4 The performance is the result of learning and practice in efficient use of physiological and psychological energy (Beashel and Taylor 1996).

Watching an élite Olympic athlete's skilled performance, it is easy to view the performance purely in terms of the physical, yet it is much more than physical movement. The skilled element in the performance forms a link between the athlete's intentions and actions. Underlying the expertise of performance is an underlying complex interaction between mental and physical processes, which is essential for all movement production. This is true irrespective of the level of performance and the age of the performer. True to say that many physical skills also contain sensory-perceptual elements, for example a child moving to receive a ball thrown to him by a friend or balancing on a set of stilts. This aspect of performance is important as the decisions made often determine the success of the action. Based on the work of Sharp (1992), Figure 3.2 illustrates that skill is more than

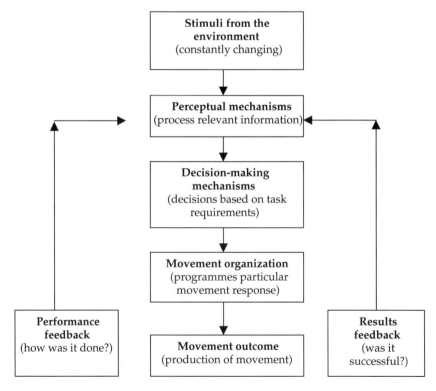

Figure 3.2 A model of human movement production.

merely carrying out certain movements and demonstrates the involvement of cognition in the endeavour.

It is beyond the scope of this text to dwell on any of these factors in detail and consequently several of the more important factors are considered.

Motivation in this context is associated with the feelings, attitudes, needs and expectations of participating in physical activity. It also has an influence on a person's decision to persevere and practise to improve their skills. In creating a positive motivational climate, attention should be paid to a number of variables, which are usefully summarized by Nichols (1990) as follows:

- Pupils must be interested in the goal towards which they are working;
- They must understand the goal to which they are working;
- Pleasant feelings associated with learning enhances motivation;
- Rewards and recognition are powerful motivators;
- Success enhances an interest in continuing to learn.

The old adage that practice makes perfect is not complete. It should be perfect practice makes perfect! In other words it is the quality of the practice that is important, rather than the time involved. Both open and closed skills benefit from practice conditions that allow the learner to practise the skill in a variety of movement conditions (Magill 1993). The variety will allow successful execution of skills in different performance situations. Skills should be practised how they are to be used and every child should have as much practice time as possible. By using different organizational formations, relationships with partners and opponents, and variety in equipment and problem-solving teaching approaches, understanding is broadened and skill enhanced. Learning is also dependent on the ability to adapt and apply previous learning. Applying what is learned in one situation to a new situation is the principle of transfer. For Nichols (1990), transfer is an integral factor in problem solving, decision making, creativity and reasoning – all vital in educating children who are informed and actively engaged in the learning experience. Teaching will be more effective if explanations relate the new skill to others already learned, to similarities in strategies in playing games and if mechanical concepts are pointed out. If children understand these relationships, they increase the chances of transferring identical or similar parts of their learning to a new skill or principle. For transfer to occur it must be taught explicitly and not left to chance (Christina and Corcos 1988).

A further factor is the provision of feedback to the child learning a skill, which Sharp (1992) claims has three purposes: to motivate; to change performance; and to reinforce learning. For simplicity, feedback can be classified as either intrinsic feedback, which is information the learner receives as a consequence of making an action (e.g. 'When I swing the bat I feel it in my hand, hear and feel it contact with the ball which I see travelling to my partner'), or extrinsic feedback, which is conveyed to the learner by an external source, normally the teacher (e.g. 'That was a super roll, Hannah. I liked the way you kept in a tucked shape during it and how you finished in a nice straight standing position at the end'). Feedback assumes that both the child and the teacher know what the correct model for the skill is and compare performance against this model of correctness. To make effective use of feedback, seek to give it in a precise way, as soon as possible after observing the action and using language that the young child will understand.

Young children as learners

Although there is research literature which has examined children's motor performances at different ages there is still much debate surrounding 'optimal readiness' and 'critical periods' for skill learning in children. Children are not 'mini adults' and need different experiences than adults. They also need these experiences offered to them in different ways. Psychological differences between adult and children learners, in particular, need to be taken into consideration and due regard given to the types of activities presented and how these may be best presented to young learners. What are these age-related differences and how do they affect the ways in which children learn motor skills?

Children become increasingly more adept at processing information as they get older, but their processing capacity is not as proficient as that of a mature person. Through experiences they strengthen their schemata, or general movement programmes. These programmes consist of commands to the muscles to make a movement response and contain information about the order, force and timing of each movement (Schmidt 1977). Young children have few experiences to call on and their schemata are not as efficient or reliable as those of adults. We know that the speed at which they process information changes as they mature, showing increase from age 3 to adolescence (Wickens 1974). Children cannot use their memory systems as effectively as adults in performing physical skills and evidence suggests that this may be due to their underdeveloped use of remembering strategies by which they can label, encode information and rehearse movement strategies (Thomas 1980). Care should be taken not to confuse learners with technical jargon or overload them with too much information at a time.

Differences in attentional capacity may also be linked to differences in experience. Whilst adults, largely through their past experiences know what are the relevant stimuli to attend to, young children are less able to identify relevant stimuli in the environment (Ross 1976). The role of the adult should be to assist in this by identifying only the important aspects, such as watching the ball when attempting a catch. Their neuromuscular control is developing and this has implications for the patterns, sequence and timing in the execution of their muscles. The more varied the movement experiences the more accurate their actions will become as they will strengthen their schemata and be more easily able to adapt to transferring this to learning new skills.

Thinking and moving

Thinking and learning are not all in our head.

(Hannaford 1995)

The human mind, and more specifically the brain, is territory that is only just being explored and discovered. Blakemore (1990) referred to it as 'the most complex piece of machinery in the universe'. The brain is not much bigger than a large grapefruit and yet it is much more powerful than any computer system. Since we were born we have possessed in our brains about 100 billion active cells called neurons (Kotulak 1996). From the earliest moments of life, these cells form new learning connections, called synapses at the rate of 3 billion every second! It is these connections that are the key to our phenomenal brain power. It is this power that is the key to our success in skilled movement production.

Normally when we think about what our minds are capable of, we may use words like thought, brain power, creativity and intelligence but see it as something as detached from our bodies. This notion is deeply rooted in our culture but it is a mistake. Research clearly indicates that the mind and body effectively act as one (Hannaford 1995; Jensen 2000). From before we are born, sensations, movements and emotions and other brain functions are inextricably linked to the body. The senses feed the brain information from the environment that helps in our understanding of the world. This is a process that begins before birth and continues into old age. Ratey (2001: 156) puts it even stronger, and states that 'movement is fundamental to the very existence of a brain'. Our movements facilitate greater cognitive function as they increase in complexity. Research in the area of the brain concerned with 'body learning', the cerebellum, has strongly linked this to cognitive processes (Parsons and Fox 1997). Movement is integral and essential to all learning. Through it we can express learning, our understanding and ourselves. The body is the medium for learning and movement is the choreography of our brain's systems.

How can our moving brain be stimulated? For over 70 years research had provided evidence of the positive effects of movement on learning (Hannaford 1995). One movement methodology is 'educational kinesiology', commonly known as 'brain gym'. Developing from work in the 1970s by Paul and Gail Dennison, this programme consists of a series of movements designed to enhance the experience of whole-brain learning. It is based on three simple premises (Dennison and Dennison 1989):

1 Learning is natural and continuous throughout life.
2 Blocks to learning occur due to an inability to move through its stress.
3 Everyone is learning-blocked to the extent we have not learned to move.

Brain gym is being used successfully by many early educators in classrooms daily, and, although lacking in substantial empirical evidence, it has received wide acclaim from those who include a movement approach to learning. Supporters claim advances in children's reading skills, thinking skills, hand–eye coordination, self-awareness and information processing abilities (Dennison and Dennison 1989). The movements themselves are intended to stimulate brain function in three dimensions: laterality (left and right hemisphere), focus (coordinating the front and back of the brain) and centring (coordinating the top and bottom of the brain). With techniques like 'lazy 8s', 'the gravity glider', 'the energy yawn' and 'thinking cap', the use of brain gym to link mind and body together for effective and long-term learning opens up huge possibilities for parents and educators alike.

Facilitating motor skill development

From birth, children are continually involved in learning different patterns of movement and new skills. We should observe this as a ladder of movement skill progression from basic actions to more specialized sports-related skills on which is placed the most important element: the child. In structuring physical education experiences, it is essential to recognize the progressive nature of movement abilities in children, so that the experiences provided are meaningful and developmentally appropriate.

The sequence of motor skill acquisition shows progression from generic movements to more complex and specialized actions. It is a process of acquisition and refinement as movements are performed with increased control and fluency (Haywood 1993). The educator should also be aware that children will pass through different levels of learning as they acquire new movement skills. Gallahue and Ozmun (1995) proposed five stages that children go through in learning a new movement skill. An adaptation of this appears in Figure 3.3.

Exploration

This is the first step on the ladder and the one where the practitioner should favour indirect instructional methods. For the young learner it is a time of pre-control. There is less emphasis on the product and more on the process. There should be less interest in how high Anneka can jump or how fast Sam can run, and more interest in children 'getting the idea' of a particular skill. Children explore the movement capabilities of their own bodies as they twist, bend, run, dodge and investigate the special properties of the hoops or skipping ropes. That is not to say that there is no concern for quality. Not at all, but success is not measured against a set speed or distance or against others, but is set within the individual's own abilities. The role of the educator is to guide and encourage in a framework where movement challenges are set in a very open-ended fashion. As the child experiments with different variations of activities, he is building a template for improved performance in skills in all movement categories.

Discovery

Here also, practitioners should use more indirect teaching methods. Guided discovery teaching, which emphasizes children finding more

Figure 3.3 The stages of learning a movement skill.

effective means of addressing the movement task is most appropriate here. There is an avoidance at this stage, too, of an overtly didactic teaching approach by the educator or an overemphasis on 'proper technique'.

This step sees the development and refinement of gross movement patterns and makes use of problem-solving scenarios that encourage the child to think about the task set and discover solutions through various means of enquiry and response. In encouraging the child to find the 'best way' how to, the guided discovery method incorporates the use of observation – peers, video, pictures and task cards. Afterwards children are given the opportunity to reassess their ideas and solutions in the light of these observations.

Combination

This step is a logical progression in the hierarchy where previously isolated movements are combined with others and experimented with in different ways. This is achieved by indirect combination (which combines activities in all the movement categories essentially using the problem-solving approaches in the earlier stages); or by direct combination (incorporating modelling correct performance, explanation and demonstration of skills). The latter method is perhaps the more traditionally recognized method of instruction in PE where children seek to replicate the model demonstrated by the leader and refine skills through practice of specific skills and integration into activities by various means.

Selection

The fourth level in the hierarchy is concerned with application, but the activities in this step are more advanced than in the combination step. Such activities include lead-up and modified games that include one or more specific skills that approximate the recognized game. The role of the educator is to assist the child to make decisions that will optimize performance in the actual game by selecting the best combination of movement skills and how best to use them. Through this, children learn to select and apply techniques in a range of sports activities that relate directly to the official version of the game with a view to improving specific performance in this activity.

Refinement

In this final step, learners put into practice previously learned skills in leisure pursuits or in competition with others. Learners by this stage are easily capable of making fine adjustments to their performances. Often these personalized adjustments will be in factors of fitness, application of body height or weight and in specific techniques within a particular sport or activity. The individual critically examines his or her strengths and weaknesses in their own level of motor skill learning through a thorough conceptualization of an individual or range of techniques. This stage epitomizes the skilled mover in PE and sport and is only seen at the highest levels of athletic performance.

The sequence of progression described is applicable to all those learning motor skills, but it should be emphasized that children in the 0–6 age range will probably be operating in the first three steps only. It is vital that time for young children is spent in exploration, discovery and combination of general movement patterns which they can enjoy and feel successful with. The role of the practitioner is to gradually extend children's movement vocabulary and the quality of movement application in a variety of activities. There is no place for the imposition of adult drills and game situations in the physical education experiences of the young child.

Teaching movement skills

Themed approaches have always been popular ways of teaching children in traditional group settings and this approach is highly recommended for teaching movement skills (Graham et al. 1993). Essentially a theme is an organizing centre around which the educator builds a lesson or series of lessons. Such an approach identifies a focus within a particular movement skill (or movement skills) and seeks to introduce or develop this within a single lesson or within a unit of work. Movement skills themes are movements that are later modified into more specialized patterns on which activities of increasing complexity are built. Once children are competent in essential core skills, these can be introduced into more complex situations, combined with other activities and adapted to meet new demands.

Examples of skills within the categories of stability, locomotion and manipulation are given in Tables 3.2, 3.3 and 3.4.

Conclusion

Children's progress in learning physical skills is rapid. Their need to acquire new skills and to improve existing ones is very much evident in those early years of their lives and this is a process that is integral to all

Table 3.2 Stability skills

	Balancing	Rolling	Dodging	Using equipment
Exploratory activities	• I want you to show me a balance on large parts of your body • Now show me a balance on smaller body parts • Can you balance a beanbag on your head and walk around the hall?	• Try to roll across your mat so quietly I cannot hear you • Roll as fast/slowly as you can • Roll forwards/sideways/backwards • Roll as low as you can get • Now roll along a straight line • Roll alongside a partner	• Dodge each other and show me a quick burst of energy • Can you dodge someone else and keep at a medium level? • Try to dodge a person chasing you from behind	• Balance on one foot while you bounce a large ball • Step along your skipping rope with both eyes closed • Stand with your feet apart and move a quoit around your body without dropping it
Discovery activities	• Why is it easier to balance on larger body parts, like our back, side or front? • Show the most difficult balance you can on three points of your body	• What do we do with our heads when we want to roll forwards? • See if you can use your hands more when you roll • How do our feet help us roll? • What can we do to help us stay still when we balance?	• What do you need to do to change direction quickly? Show me • Do you find it easier to dodge in one direction? • Try dodging a friend chasing you. What do you do to help yourself?	• As you walk along a bench, concentrate on using your arms to help you balance • Use the horizontal ladder to hang from. Is it better to look down or straight ahead? Why?

Table 3.2 Continued

	Balancing	Rolling	Dodging	Using equipment
Combination activities	• Move along the climbing frame showing balances at two different levels • Make up a sequence of three actions on the floor; and include two different balances	• In the next roll I want you to start from a wide base and finish in a narrow base • Do three forward rolls along the bench one after the other • Try to roll across your mat while holding a ball	• Dodge more than two people while running across the playground • Dodge a ball rolled at you from a low level • Repeat at a high level	• Combine three travelling actions on the rope ladders • Use three different actions to make up a short dance. Repeat this twice

Table 3.3 Locomotor skills

	Jumping	Skipping	Galloping	Climbing
Exploratory activities	• Jump and land as lightly/heavily as you can • Can you jump up and touch the same spot three times? • Use little bounces and jump the first letter of your name • Jump into/out of the hoop	• Skip landing heavily on one foot and lightly on the other. Change feet • How many skips does it take you to go across the playground? • Can you skip in a circle? • Try to skip while holding a friend's hand	• Gallop around the hall as if escaping from a wild animal • Can you gallop with one leg stiff? Change legs • Gallop forwards/backwards • Try to gallop taking big/small steps	• Can you climb along/around/over the apparatus? • Climb and use your feet in different ways • Climb over the apparatus linked to a partner by a short rope
Discovery activities	• Jump straight up into the air. What happens if you don't use your arms too? • What happens to your body in the air when you jump up? • Tell me what happens to your knees when you land	• Skip around the hall using large and small steps. When would you want to use each of these? • Find out what your legs do when you skip • Watch a partner and describe their skipping	• Gallop around the hall with different feet leading. Which is easier for you? • How can your arms help when you gallop? • Try different amounts of knee bend when galloping	• Climb across the bars using different grips. What difference does this make? • If you wanted to climb to the top of the rope quickly, how would you do it? • Find three ways to use your hands to climb

Table 3.3 Continued

	Jumping	Skipping	Galloping	Climbing
Combination activities	• Jump once for distance and once for height • Jump as fast and as far as you can • Jump, turn, land and roll	• Can you skip as quietly as possible and make yourself as small as you can? • Make up a chasing game that involves skipping	• Gallop for eight steps in one direction, then eight in another. Repeat twice • Gallop in a straight line while bouncing a ball	• Climb along the horizontal ladder using different grips • Using all the ways of climbing you know, climb across the apparatus

Table 3.4 Manipulative actions

	Kicking	Catching	Rolling	Striking
Exploratory activities	• Kick the ball so it goes very slowly/quickly • Kick the ball with your right/left leg • Kick and keep the ball as low to the ground as you can • Kick a small ball to a partner	• Can you catch with your hands in different positions? • Catch a beanbag from a sitting/lying position • Try to catch a ball thrown from the side • Catch a ball not using your hands	• Roll a ball as slow/fast as possible • Roll a hoop across the playground • Roll a quoit to a partner a short distance away • Try to roll a ball so that it curves	• Hit a ball so that it makes a loud noise • Strike a ball from a low level to a high level • Use your hand to strike a ball coming towards you • Hit a small ball through two cones • Hit a ball like your partner
Discovery activities	• Kick your ball without bending your leg. What happens? • Which part of your foot helped you kick the ball high into the air? • Do we use our arms to help us kick? How?	• Show me four different ways to catch a quoit • What do your arms do when you catch? Show me • Try to catch a ball thrown hard and one thrown softly. Which was easier?	• Find three different ways to roll a small ball • What should we do to make the ball go as straight as possible • Roll the same ball on different surfaces. What happens?	• Try hitting a balloon, then a ball. Is it different? • Strike a small ball from a tee. Compare to hitting a ball that is thrown • Stand in different ways to strike a ball coming at you

Table 3.4 Continued

	Kicking	Catching	Rolling	Striking
Combination activities	• Kick the ball three times, showing a different amount of force each time • Kick to a moving target • Play kicking rounders	• Jump up into the air and catch a ball at waist level • Catch five different objects thrown to you • Make up a catching game with a friend	• Try to roll a large ball with different amounts of force • Roll a ball and mirror your partner's technique • Play skittles	• Strike a ball with a bat as hard as you can to travel to a partner at a low level • Use two different bats and the same swing each time • Play French cricket

humans. Dispositions to want to learn and experiences of learning and improving skills such as walking, running, throwing or climbing are significant in the development of other skills throughout our lives. For practitioners and educators, some knowledge of skill acquisition and development is vital in ensuring that the experiences are enjoyable, valuable and will allow children to lead active and full lives. In the following chapter the importance of physical activity in the lives of young children is considered.

4

Observing children's movements

Active children perform many movement skills. An understanding of how to observe these is also a valuable skill.

The children in a reception class have been listening to the story *Going on a Bear Hunt* on tape. They have been encouraged to make different movements to accompany the story line and have shown imagination in their various actions. The class teacher has observed the variety of movements and wishes to make her observations more systematic so that she can help the children develop their movements. How can she best be supported here? What methods of observations are preferable on this occasion? What are the important features she needs to observe in the movements of the children?

Introduction

Paul Dennison, creator of *Brain Gym* (Dennison and Dennison 1989), wrote that movement was the key to learning and as advances in neuroscience reveal new relationships between the mind and body these are constant reminders of the significance of movement in the acquisition of knowledge and skills. Carla Hannaford took a similar view when she wrote that movement 'is essential to the learning process to allow children to explore every aspect of movement and balance in their environment, whether walking on a curb, climbing a tree, or jumping on the furniture' (1995: 101).

Human movement certainly does manifest itself in many ways and such versatility is characteristic of the human species. We can observe it in the cries and sounds of a baby expressing needs and feelings in movement to the aesthetic excellence of a trained dancer at the very pinnacle of their art. We see it in the creative impulse of the artist on canvas and in the controlled mastery of the gymnast. It is so much a feature of our everyday lives, young and old and is an index of feelings and personality. It is most definitely 'an abundant product of being alive' (Department for Education and Science 1972: 3).

In order to guide children's movements, an understanding of movement and how to observe it accurately is vital. In Chapter 3 the idea of movement skill themes for promoting development in motor skills was introduced. This chapter focuses on movement concepts, which are the dynamic qualities used to colour the range and effectiveness of a given skill.

Understanding movement concepts

Developed from frameworks originating from Laban (1947), four essential components of movement can be identified; namely 'body awareness' (what the body can do), 'space' (where the body moves), 'effort' (how the body moves), and 'relationships' (with whom or what the body moves) (see Figure 4.1).

Body awareness

This refers to the ability to know what actions the body is capable of doing and understand how these actions are performed. Included are actions from all three categories of movement; stability, locomotion and manipulation. Within each of these skill themes more specific actions can be seen. These include whole body actions, actions of specific body parts, and body shapes in the movement skills of running, jumping, swinging, rolling, throwing and striking. Activities involving locomotion should progress from movement in free space to actions that require more control and the utilization of objects. Stability actions are vital because before children can move, they must be able to support themselves in a stable way. Activities should concentrate on balancing, stretching, swinging, pulling and lifting. Manipulation involves imparting force to objects, controlling and

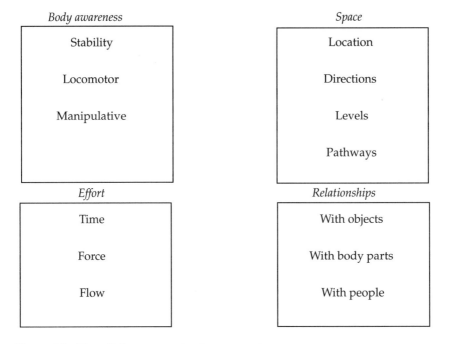

Figure 4.1 Essential components of movement.

sustaining control of different objects. Activities in this category should complement the development of stability and locomotor skills and are introduced simultaneously.

The following activities are designed to develop body awareness:

- Balance on one foot. Reach up with both arms overhead, now to the side and then to the ground
- Gallop (slide) opposite a partner keeping time with each other
- Can you catch a ball with body parts other than your hands? Show me
- Join two rolls together. The first one as fast and the second as slowly as you can
- Laterality is also essential and movement tasks should be devised to develop understanding in unilateral, bilateral and cross-lateral movements (Thomas *et al.* 1988), such as:
  - Walk like a bear. Use the arm and leg on the same side of your body together to move.
  - Perform three bunny hops in a row.
  - Can you move like an alligator? Use one hand and the opposite leg to move at the same time.

Space

Spatial awareness is sensing where the body moves in space and since all movement takes place in space, children who understand about space will be better able to move safely through the different environments in physical education. Five categories define the aspects of space:

- self-space
- general space
- directions
- levels
- pathways.

Self-space is the immediate space children have around themselves and general space is the larger area in which they can operate. This larger area is the space in the hall, the outdoor area that the body can move through by means of locomotion. This aspect should be taught earliest in the programme as it is the base on which all movement is built. Directions, are the dimensional possibilities that the space offers. This can be up/down, forwards/backwards, right/left and clockwise/anticlockwise. Levels can be divided into high (above shoulder height), medium (between the knees and the shoulders) or low (below knee height). There are three pathways possible in space – straight, curvy and zig-zag. Movements here may be on the floor or through the air.

Extensions are the size of movement in the space, such as windmill actions with large arm circles, or the distance from the centre of the body that the parts reach to perform a movement, such as maintaining a small tucked shape when rolling.

The following activities will help children understand about spatial awareness:

• Pretend you have a terrible itch in the middle of your back that you need to scratch! Stay in your own space and stretch, curl and twist your body in different directions to scratch it.
• Imagine yourself as a paintbrush. I want you to pretend to paint the inside of the hall in your favourite colour. Make sure you don't miss any spaces!
• Hop forwards. Walk backwards slowly. Can you slide from side to side like a skater? Now jump up and down as though you are using a pogo stick.
• Move around the whole space. When you hear the drum beat change to moving at a low level. When it beats again, move around with one part of your body at a high level.
• Bounce around the hall in zig-zag lines. Use the same action but in curvy lines only. What is the difference?

Effort

This defines how the body moves. It can be divided into the three components of time, force and flow. Often this aspect of movement is neglected, being seen as somewhat vague unlike an action such as kicking a ball where the end product is easily observable. It is essential that children understand this dynamic and can apply it in their various actions. Movement can be deemed skilful through selection of the right combination of these qualities. Children can be taught to understand about time by contrasts in the extremes, e.g. fast and slow. Progressing work along the time continuum will assist children being able to execute movement actions at different speeds depending on the requirements of a particular task. Force is related to the amount of energy expended to execute a movement. As with time, teaching extremes in performing actions lightly or strongly will develop understanding here. Activities may be performed using the whole body, for example running, or with certain body parts only, such as striking with a bat. Finally in this category is flow. This is the amount of control within a movement and it ranges from free to bound.

Free flow is continuous movement that is not halted after the action has begun. An example of this is the forward roll where once begun, it is virtually impossible to stop the movement!

Bound flow movements, by contrast, are those under the control of the performer and who is able to stop them at any time. Examples of such movements are walking, skipping, hopping, jumping actions that can be initiated at any time by the performer.

Here are some further activities to teach about effort:

- Run fast. When I clap my hands I want you to run as slowly as you can.
- Walk around the space like a giant with heavy plodding steps. Can you tiptoe around as lightly as you can. Try not to make any noise at all.
- Can you move like a wooden soldier? Now move like a rag doll. Tell me how your movements are different.
- Use a bat to strike the small ball as hard as you can. Try to do the same again but this time hit it with as little force as you can.
- Listen to these three words in this sentence, 'Run, jump, balance.' Do each action and try to make the movements as flowing as you can. Can you make up another movement sentence with actions that flow too?

Relationships

This concept defines with whom or with what the body moves and involves the variables of the whole body, body parts and objects in simultaneous interaction. Movement with the whole body may be seen with individuals and groups. For example, a child in moving around the working space relates to others moving around, between, over, under or alongside another child or a group of children. An individual is able to follow and match the movements of another or provide contrasting movements. In the same way, a group of children may move in relationship to a single child. Relationships focusing on body parts involve initial identification of these and it is imperative that young children have a functional vocabulary for the names of body parts. Once this has been established, the focus of the unit of work may shift to making shapes with the parts (i.e. narrow, wide, long, thin and twisted) or using them in relation to each other (e.g. travelling on, changing shape during, etc.). By using a variety of objects, basic actions can be refined or varied. Consider the skill theme of throwing. Resources need to be varied and these would include quoits, beanbags, shuttlecocks, foam javelins, beach balls, balloons or airflow balls. The task set might be, 'What is the best way to throw this particular object?' Children will need to select the best motor programme available to solve this movement problem (Thomas *et al.* 1988). With practice their motor programmes become more automatic and their selection of response becomes quicker and more accurate.

These activities foster learning about relationships:

- Point to the ceiling with your right elbow. Do the same with your left knee.
- How quickly can you touch the ground with your right hand? Your left heel? Your right thigh?
- Use two different body parts to move around the hall. Practise this and show a friend.
- Explore the equipment in front of you. I want you to travel over it in any way you can. Now travel around it with the same action. Finally try to have as many body parts as far away from the equipment as possible.
- Stand opposite a partner. When the music plays do the same actions as each other at the same time. This is called mirroring. Can you both make up a short sequence of movements together?

The process of observing

Sharon helps out three mornings a week in a local playgroup. Twelve children attend this regularly. She has been working there for two months and enjoys interacting with the children and working alongside them. She has learned so much about them as individuals merely by watching them over this short time, but she would like to find out more so she can be even more effective in helping each child to learn and develop. What are the best ways to observe young children? Who shall she choose to observe and for how long? How will her observations inform her about the nature of the children's learning?

The importance of observation for early years educators is recognized by many. Hurst and Joseph (1998: 63) sum this up admirably when they write, 'good education in the early years rests on the ability of practitioners to understand children's development and to learn from observation how to use their knowledge and understanding to further individual children's learning in an educational setting'. Similarly, Ofsted (1996) reported that acute observation skills, good judgements, clear feedback along with thoughtful and sharp comments, were all contributors to effective performance and progress in pupils' understanding.

Movement, due to its transitory nature, is no easy thing to observe analytically. When children paint a picture, make music, write or build a model the tangible evidence of this is clearly in evidence. Yet the importance of observing and recording it is not disputed. Maude endorses this importance in saying that, 'Movement observation is an invaluable tool in constant use by children and their teachers. Movement observation also becomes an ability which, if developed and used effectively in conjunction with assessment and feedback, can vastly enhance children's achievements' (2001: 67).

Children as observers

Thomas *et al*. (1988) identify three types of subjects for children to watch. First, children can observe other children. Peer observation is an important tool for the physically educated children to have. Children do watch other children and in this process they are continually comparing, contrasting and evaluating their actions. Expect to hear phrases such as, 'Jane's roll was good. It was quicker than mine', or 'I want to balance on one leg like Amanda'. From the outset, however, children need to be exposed to quality. This can be provided by the adult, another child or through video playback of other children. Once the salient features of quality in a particular performance are highlighted, children should be able to identify these characteristics in the movements of others. If children cannot observe the key points in a skill they will also be unable to teach each other effectively since neither will know which components of the skill to correct. Children need to recognize what the difference is between good and poor quality movement and begin to articulate these differences to others.

Second, children observe the teacher or adult as a model. The use of demonstration in movement contexts is a powerful model indeed (Magill 1993). In addition to modelling good technique, children observing adults learn other information that can foster their skill development. For example they will be asking themselves questions such as, 'Does my teacher like me?', 'Does she think I have good skills?' or 'Can I do my best throw when my teacher is watching?' A teacher/practitioner, carer or parent can develop understanding further by providing praise and encouragement and by discussing observations with children.

The final aspect of children as observers has to do with children as self-assessors. From infancy, children observe, evaluate and assess their performance across a range of motor skills. Although not always beneficial to their learning, with guidance it is an important part of skill acquisition and development. Adults need to inform children about what to look for in evaluating their own performances and, as their observation skills improve, more can be expected in their responses to their self-assessments.

You might hear, for example, 'I didn't catch the ball because my hands were too far apart'.

Adults as observers

Observation by adults is a common feature in early childhood settings. Often this may be to evaluate a programme, to determine the appropriateness of learning objectives or teaching effectiveness, to assess and determine progress (Thomas *et al.* 1988). Such procedures have become daily practice, yet little is known about how to become a good observer. What specifically should the adult look for in observing children's motor skills? Are there preferred techniques for observing children moving? Hobart and Frankel (1994) provide helpful guidance and propose a number of observation techniques appropriate for use with young children. The five techniques described below, with their respective advantages and disadvantages, should provide a useful starting point for observing children's movement skills.

Written record
This is perhaps the most commonly used technique for observing children. It is simply a written description of what is happening as you observe. Written in the present tense it records noteworthy events as they happen.

Advantages: It is a skill already in existence. Little preparation is necessary.

Disadvantages: It cannot record every detail. It may become repetitive.

Checklists
These are of much benefit in separating children's physical development from other aspects of development. Although there are a number of published checklists available, it is also feasible to devise one's own to suit the particular context in which one is working.

Advantages: They record a lot of information quickly. Results are easy to read and understand.

Disadvantages: Care must be taken to preserve objectivity. If the child is unwell or unmotivated on the day, recording may be affected.

Movement charts
These are a useful way of presenting information about the movements of more than one child. They can be used to track a group of children's movements within a classroom or nursery setting, or indeed tracking particular movements during an outdoor play session.

Advantages: Provides information on use of equipment.

Disadvantages: Not sufficiently detailed.

Digital photographs

These are increasingly used for a variety of purposes but with huge potential for capturing snapshots of children moving. Permission must be obtained from the parent or carer before this technique can be used.

Advantages: Accurate record of movement possible. Allows for post-action analysis. Valuable as a diagnostic tool.

Disadvantages: Difficult to get quality pictures. May affect children adversely.

Video-recording

Video-recording is also used with increased popularity. It can be used to capture movements of a large group or class, or the specific movements of a single child. Permission must be obtained from the parent or carer before this technique can be used also.

Advantages: Very portable. Accurate record of movements possible. Valuable evidence of movement capability.

Disadvantages: Technical difficulties.

Assessing movement

> Assessment is an important and integral part of any good quality early years provision.
>
> (Heald 1998: 20)

Heald's claim is certainly true, but assessment is a term that remains less than well defined in the literature. Indeed, Satterly (1989) describes it as 'an omnibus term', which relates to describing children's learning, the relationship to teaching aims and the environment designed to facilitate learning. Assessment is central to children's learning in any domain, and as Carroll (1994) suggests, it is an integral part of teaching and learning. The reasons for assessing reflect this:

- To identify what children know, can do and understand;
- To give feedback;
- To identify individual needs;
- To motivate;

- To assist in target setting;
- To provide information for others (parents, carers, teachers, etc.);
- To evaluate provision;
- To inform future planning.

In assessing children's growth, development and motor behaviours, the use of specific tests has been included in general child development batteries since the 1920s. Gabbard (1992) reports that early tests tended to focus on the quantitative characteristics of ability (i.e. how far, how fast, how many) or on more general assessments, which involved asking a child if she could balance on one foot, stack a number of cubes or kick a ball. Although providing some valid and reliable data, such information is limited in describing the process of change over time. More recent instruments have centred on the qualitative characteristics of motor behaviour.

Examples of standardized tests of motor development and movement capability include:

- The Brazelton Behavioural Assessment Scale (Brazelton 1984) is often administered to babies for whom there is some cause for concern and which incorporates assessment of reflex actions.
- Bayley Scales of Infant Development (Bayley 1993) include a psychomotor development index assessing both gross and fine movement actions.
- The Bruininks-Oseretsky Test for Motor Proficiency (Bruininks 1978) consists of 46 items of motor proficiency and separate scores for fine and gross motor abilities.
- The Test of Gross Motor Development (Ulrich 1985), used with children from the age of 3 years, represents an easily administered assessment of the most common locomotor and manipulative motor skills.
- Fundamental Movement Pattern Assessment Instrument (McClenaghan and Gallahue 1978) is an observation instrument designed to assess changes in movement pattern over time. It includes assessment of five fundamental movement skills – running, jumping, throwing, catching and kicking.

Although some of the available tests are used to document change in motor abilities, observation is a more immediate way to assess movement skills. Observation and evaluation of movements seen in a practical context are inextricably linked in physical education. Spackman (1998) has suggested that this connection contributes to a teacher's extensive knowledge of a child's strengths and weaknesses. Direct observation is the best way of assessing young children, but in order to assess, one has to know what to look for in movement responses since observation for assessment purposes is much more than merely watching a child. Here there is an expectation that the observer will learn about a child's abilities as a result of their observations over a period of time. Inevitably this will involve the use of criteria against which movement can be assessed. The following criteria are offered not as definite answers but as possible starting points for further development.

Gross motor skills

Is the child able to:

1 Crawl/climb?
2 Balance comfortably on one leg for 5 seconds?
3 Walk along a straight line with a heel to toe action?
4 Bounce a large ball with one hand?
5 Run around the space safely without bumping into anyone?
6 Catch a large ball consistently with two hands?
7 Jump with both feet together and land balanced on both feet?
8 Stop and start quickly when travelling?
9 Hop equally well on either leg?
10 Bend, twist and stretch the body
11 Gallop with either the left or right foot leading?
12 Skip to a point and back in a smooth and rhythmic action?

Fine motor skills

Is the child able to:

1 Open and close each hand independently?
2 Touch fingers to thumb on each hand?
3 Rotate each wrist to turn palms up/downwards?
4 (Un)fasten buttons on own clothing?
5 Tie shoelaces and fasten buckles on shoes?
6 Use a knife and fork to eat with?
7 Build a tower of at least five bricks?
8 Cut out shapes using scissors held in one hand?
9 Hold a cup without spilling the contents?
10 Colour inside shapes with some accuracy?
11 Trace over/write under own name?
12 Screw and unscrew plastic nuts and bolts in construction sets?

Planning to observe and assess

The key to becoming a skilled observer is, as with other skills, through practice and more practice! From the outset it is important to know exactly what will be the focus of the observation. It could be, for instance, how one particular technique is performed or the confidence displayed by the children in performing it. A second consideration is that of knowing exactly what the key features of the skill are. In observing skipping, for example, the observer should be aware of how the arms are used in the movement, identify how weight is transferred throughout, the coordination between the step and hop and the balance on the toes on landing. These are the critical observational cues for this skill. By trying a range of observational techniques it will quickly become apparent whether the technique chosen is appropriate and suits the observer. This is also true when recording observations. Try different formats until you are comfortable with a system. With practice, not only will the children's movement skills improve, but your skill as an observer will also improve!

Barrett (1984) provides guidance on planning to observe children in movement settings. The model is based on three principles. *Analysis* – knowing the critical features of the skill with understanding of the mechanical principles involved in its proficient performance. *Planning* – understanding the importance of planning and organizing the observations with a clear focus. *Positioning* – commonly this involves a front, middle and side view and the value of the observer moving around to watch the performer from these different angles.

An adaptation of this model is shown below:

1 *Describe the setting:* Give information on the number and age of the children, facilities, equipment and the children's prior experiences.
2 *State the task:* This sets out what the children will be specifically involved in for the purpose of the observation.
3 *Decide on a focus:* In advance analyse the movements you're going to be observing and identify the key features of these.
4 *Determine the length of the observation:* This may be only several minutes or may involve a lengthier time frame within a lesson.
5 *Select a technique:* Choose one of the techniques of observation that will best capture the information you seek. Supporting strategies will involve scanning to obtain a general picture, and focusing to obtain more detailed information on an individual child.
6 *Position yourself:* Positioning yourself around the perimeter of the working area and bringing an individual to you for more detailed study allows you to gather the necessary information with a minimum of disruption.

Observing movement skill themes

Running

Running is a more advanced skill than walking although the mechanics of running are similar to walking. Haywood distinguishes between the two in this way, 'running has a period of "flight" when neither foot is touching the ground; in walking, one foot is always in contact with the ground' (1993: 128). Alongside the airborne phase in running, this skill is also characterized by speed of action, a longer stride and the use of the arms to add power to the whole movement.

What you *should* see: head is up, body leans forward; knees bend and swing forward and up; arm action in opposition to leg action; a definite airborne phase; support leg is extended.

What you *might* see: head down, exaggerated lean; awkward action, not flowing; arms flop out to the sides; little flight, flat-footed landing; lower leg waves in or out.

Recommendations

- Allow children to recognize how their running changes in general space.
- Use changes of direction (forward, backwards, sideways).
- Get them to explore running in different pathways.
- Ask them to vary the speed and force of their runs.
- Vary running for distance and running at speed.
- Let them experience running in relation to objects and other children.

Jumping

Wickstrom (1983: 65) defines jumping as 'a motor skill in which the body is propelled into the air by a thrust from one or both legs and then lands on one or both feet'. This definition also embraces hopping, leaping and bounding actions. A jump may be performed in upward, downward, forward, backward or sideways directions and using the foot or feet in different ways to take off from or land on. The information below relates to a jump in a vertical direction.

What you *should* see: crouch position before take-off; a powerful extension of the legs; arms reach forward and upwards; body is fully extended in flight; soft landing, flexed knees and ankles.

What you *might* see: little or no preparatory crouch; inability to take off from two feet; arm movements are restricted; failure to extend fully on take-off; landing on one foot, off balance.

Recommendations

- Begin with exploratory activities and progress to directed techniques later.
- Make sure children are wearing appropriate shoes and socks.
- Allow jumping on soft surfaces only, e.g. grass, mats.
- Encourage an exploding action with strong take-off.
- Illustrate the coordinated use of arms and legs together.
- Teach a 'give' position on landing. Seek balances finishes.

Climbing

Cratty (1979) reports that newborn infants show a reflex similar to vertical climbing and later development would seem to be associated with achieving an upright position and early attempts at walking. Gallahue (1982) believes it is a fundamental movement that begins around the time an infant learns to creep, indeed a child's first climbing experiences usually involve ascending and descending stairs. Later movements can be observed in climbing apparatus in local parks and in more structured gymnastics lessons in school.

What you *should* see: strong grip on the apparatus; comfortably managing body weight; smooth and fluent motion; opposite arm–leg action in use; confidence.

What you *might* see: weak grip, thumbs around bar; struggling to hold own weight; slow and jerky progress; same arm–leg action; nervousness, reluctance.

Recommendations

- Begin with exploratory activities but assess entry skill levels.
- Supervise carefully, instilling confidence in the climber.
- Teach children to wrap their thumbs around the bar at all times.
- Demonstrate how one hand and opposite leg move at the same time.
- Encourage a follow grasp and/or follow step action.
- Remind children that the hand and leg movements are similar to the creeping and crawling actions of a baby.

Throwing

This is a ballistic skill like kicking or striking in which force is applied to an object to propel it over a distance. The mechanical principles involved in projecting objects from a strike, throw or a kick are similar. Styles of throwing vary and commonly involve underarm, overarm and sideways. Haywood (1993) suggests that the ballistic skill that researchers have studied most is the overarm throw for distance. This is the skill for consideration here.

What you *should* see: arm swung back in preparation; opposite arm held out to balance; step forward on opposite foot; weight is transferred forward; body faces target on release; throwing arm follows through in the direction of the throw.

What you *might* see: little attempt at a backswing; non-throwing arm redundant; same arm, same leg action; little transference of weight; body position away from target; inability to release the object in the desired direction/trajectory.

Recommendations

- Begin by concentrating on throwing for distance, then on speed and finally on accuracy.
- Encourage speed of movement and hip rotation at an early stage.
- Use a variety of throwing objects such as beanbags, balls, quoits, frisbees, foam javelins, etc.
- Have hoops or carpet squares as cues to encourage stepping out on the opposite foot to throw.
- Provide as many opportunities as possible to practise the skill.

Striking with a bat

This is a complex motor skill for children to learn that encompasses already familiar skills. It involves learning to drop an object accurately so that it may be contacted, visually tracking the object through the air and making contact with it at exactly the correct moment. Graham *et al.* (1993: 413) give two main reasons for its complexity. They indicate that visual tracking is a skill that develops in children throughout their primary school years and that hand–eye coordination away from the body is difficult. It is an important skill, however, with later applications to a number of sporting activities such as rounders, golf, tennis and volleyball.

What you *should* see: bat is held up ready; trunk is turned to the side;

weight transfers to the front foot; eyes watch the ball all the time; strike occurs in a long horizontal plane.

What you *might* see: no anticipation of a strike; body remains front facing; little or no weight shift; eyes not following the object; swing is short and abrupt.

Recommendations

- Follow an instructional progression that begins with striking with the hand, using other body parts, to short-handled implements and finally long-handled implements.
- Consider using balloons and large beach balls initially. Begin with large objects and progress to smaller objects.
- Practise hitting stationary objects before moving ones.
- Work on transfer of weight and a level swing. Tell children to 'Keep your eyes on the ball'.
- Remember the influence of the colour of the background and the object to be struck on the figure–ground perception of the batter.

Conclusion

In this chapter we have emphasized the need for and the importance of observing children's movements. Active children perform many movement skills and for those concerned with assisting their physical development and skill improvement, an understanding of how to observe is in itself a valued skill. By identifying what skill is to be observed, what features of it should be observed and some thought given to how and when the observation(s) will take place, the observer can soon become quite adept and consequently the interactions with the children will benefit too. It is also a skill that every child should be encouraged to develop. In the next chapter, the theme of including all children in activity and physical education is developed with recommendations given of how this may be put into practice.

5

Movement education for all

Meeting the diverse needs of all children presents a challenge for parents, carers and educators.

Introduction

The fundamental principle of the inclusive school is that all children should learn together, wherever possible, regardless of any difficulties or differences they may have. Inclusive schools must recognise and respond to the diverse needs of their students, accommodating both different styles of learning and ensuring quality education to all through appropriate curricula, organisational arrangements, teaching strategies, resources use and partnership with their communities. There should be a continuum of special needs encountered by every school.

(UNESCO 1994: 11)

It has been argued throughout this book that movement, physical activity and play are central features of children's lives. They create a context for learning that goes far beyond physical skills. In Bruner's words, they represent the 'culture of childhood' (1983: 121). Physical education is the only area of the child's curriculum specifically related to movement, and as such, it ought to lie at the very heart of every child's schooling.

This chapter discusses an 'inclusive' approach to movement experiences; an approach that aims to provide positive, rewarding and challenging movement experiences for all children, irrespective of their ability. It does so within the context of on-going debates within education and society about the rights of children, in general and of those with special needs, in particular.

Moving towards inclusion

Inclusion is not about placing children in mainstream schools. It is about changing schools to make them more responsive to the needs of all children. It is about helping all teachers to accept responsibility for the learning of all children in their school and preparing them to teach those children who are currently excluded from their school, for whatever reason.

(Mittler 2000: vii–viii)

Inclusion, special needs, disability, handicap. For many years, the language used to describe children with different abilities has been a topic of intense debate. The most frequently used term in recent years, within the context of school provision, has been Special Educational Needs. This phrase dates back to the 1960s, when it reflected an increasing dissatisfaction with the language of 'handicap', and a recognition that the system of separate education was failing many pupils with physical or learning difficulties, both in their educational experience and their social and personal development (Oliver 1996). The highly influential Warnock Report (Department for Education and Science 1978) was an attempt to address these issues in the United Kingdom. It rejected the notion that there are two types of children: those with and those without a handicap, and stressed that whether or not a child's condition constitutes an educational handicap depended on many factors, such as the school's expertise and resources, the pupils' personality, the quality of support, and the encouragement within the family and community. It was considered entirely conceivable that a pupil with a disability could, in many contexts, perform as well or better than peers, given appropriate support. By focusing on a pupil's 'need', rather than a 'handicap', the emphasis shifted from a mere description to a statement of the educational help and provision required.

Whilst there is little doubt that the language of special needs is a marked improvement on that of handicap, many recent thinkers and writers have complained that standard language remains problematic: the very idea of special educational needs implies separation, difference and abnormality. Jean Gross (1996), for example, argues that a Special Educational Need was originally something a child *had*, but it has often come to mean something that the child *is*. In other words, special needs are used to label certain children in much the same way that handicap did a generation before. It is in the context of such debates that the notion of 'inclusion' has come to the fore.

A number of recent debates in the area of special needs/inclusion seem to centre on different ideas of disability. Mike Oliver (1996) has been highly influential in highlighting a distinction between what he calls 'individual' and 'social' models of disability. A reliance on the individual model, he argues, lies at the heart of inappropriate provision for disabled people. The 'problem' of disability, according to this model, is located within the individual, and the causes of this problem stem from some impairment or limitation that is assumed to arise from disability. Underpinning these assumptions is a view of disability as some personal tragedy. The social model, on the other hand, denies that individual limitations or losses are the causes of the problem. Rather, it is located within society, and its failure to meet the needs of a particular group. So, the social model upholds the view that it is society which disables individuals, not any impairment they may have.

It is for these reasons, amongst others, that many educators and policy makers have started to refer to Inclusive, rather than Special Education. This is more than a simple change in terminology, since it reflects a conviction that nothing short of a radical reappraisal of the structure and character of schooling is needed if it is to adequately meet the needs of all its pupils (see Jenkinson 1997). These views certainly have an important international reference point in The Salamanca Statement, from which the quote at the start of this chapter was taken.

Changing teaching and learning in physical education

What does this mean for physical education? Certainly, there will be a need for innovative and creative thinking on the part of teachers and early years practitioners. Mike Blamires (1999) has argued that inclusion is fundamentally concerned with access and engagement with one's peers in tasks that are at an appropriate level and worthwhile. In practice, this seems most likely to occur when practitioners and settings interpret their role with versatility, offering a range of provision, to meet the range of needs of the children involved.

Perhaps the move towards an increasingly inclusive model of schooling demands a more radical reappraisal of the content and purpose of physical education than many have fully recognized. For example, Len Barton (1993) has questioned whether the physical education curriculum that all pupils are entitled to access is premised on an enabling view of disability. He argues that important issues still need to be considered if all pupils are really going to participate on an equal basis with their able-bodied peers. Barton's (1993: 49) charges include the following:

- Physical education is the creation of and for able-bodied people.
- It gives priority to certain types of human movement.
- The motivation to participate is encouraged through the articulations of idealized notions of 'normality'.

Even if these accusations are only partly justified, it is difficult to deny that traditional conceptions of physical education and activity require a fundamental rethink.

Two consequences of a properly inclusive approach to physical education need stressing at this point. First, teaching practices will need redesigning. Second, the organization of learning will have to become infinitely more flexible than it is at present (Bailey and Robertson 2000). If children with different abilities are to learn together, then the practitioner needs to consider strategies to adapt aspects of the activity to best meet their needs. This is usually referred to as differentiation, and is the topic of the next section.

Differentiation

> Teaching is teaching, regardless of the range of needs of pupils, and an essential prerequisite of integration in the new sense of the word is the acquisition of a commitment on the part of teachers to work with all children, whether they have special needs or not.
>
> (Oliver 1996: 87)

Children come into school, or playgroup or nursery with a wide range of talents, needs and interests. Some are faster, some are slower; some love to run and jump and twist and turn at any opportunity, others have a more controlled style of physical activity; some turn up already showing signs of very high ability in some sort of activity; others seem to struggle from the start to keep up with their peers. This diversity of needs and abilities presents one of the evident challenges confronting the adults who work with young children; it also presents one of the greatest sources of satisfaction.

Differentiation is the term used to refer to ways that teachers try to meet the different needs of children. It involves planning to meet the range of needs within a class as effectively as possible, in order to maximize the achievements of each individual child. It takes place when some aspect of a session is changed to better reflect the abilities and needs that the learners bring to the situation.

The model of differentiation that we discuss in this book (originally presented in Bailey 2000b) is based on the presumption that adults, when preparing to work with a group of children, make three main sorts of decisions. These are not the only decisions that they make. However, they are among the most important, especially with regard to the way that the practitioner expects a lesson or a series of lessons to progress. So, by thinking a little about these decisions, the practitioner is better able to meet the needs of the different children, with their different abilities, in the class or group.

The key to effective differentiation is planning, and this is likely to become more effective and focused as familiarity with a group of children grows. An experienced teacher or carer will know the individual characters, strengths and weaknesses of the children in the group, and will know the different ways to strike a balance between ease and difficulty of tasks. Others will be less familiar with their group. A useful approach during these early lessons is to begin with tasks that are likely to challenge the majority ability range, but also plan variations to those tasks for children with higher and lower abilities, and intervene with them if it becomes clear that certain pupils need some help. Increased familiarity with a class allows for more precise planning and differentiation.

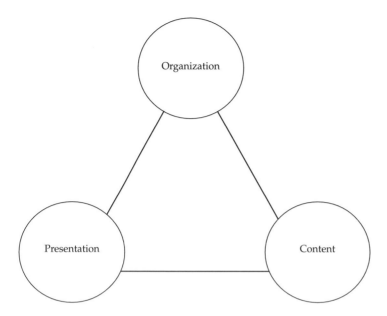

Figure 5.1 A model for differentiation.

The basic model of differentiation considered here is represented in Figure 5.1.

According to this model, the teacher makes a series of decisions that determine the character of the lesson. Each corner of the triangle – organization, presentation and content – relates to a different aspect of the lesson. By making decisions about these aspects, the teacher is in a position to differentiate to meet the needs of the learners. These decisions are made within the contexts both of teaching the class as a whole and the individuals within that class.

Teachers and carers make these sorts of decisions all of the time when they work with young children. There is nothing special or profound about them. For example, when you think about a lesson or group of lessons, you are very likely to ask yourself something like this:

What am I going to teach these children? CONTENT
What is the best way to teach them? PRESENTATION
How shall I arrange them? ORGANIZATION

Similarly, if it transpires that an individual or group has some problems during the lesson, the source of their problems may very well turn out to be associated with the same three variables:

The work is too easy or challenging for the children. CONTENT
They do not understand what to do. PRESENTATION
They are being disrupted by others in the group. ORGANIZATION

All this model of differentiation aims to do is make these sorts of thoughts and decisions more explicit and clear, and in doing so make it easier for teachers to meet the needs of all of the children in their care. The distinction between organization, presentation and content might, in itself, provide a useful way of thinking through planning and teaching. But it is also possible to take matters a little further, by breaking up the three types of decisions into sub-themes, and in doing so, move towards more specific strategies for differentiation (see Figure 5.2).

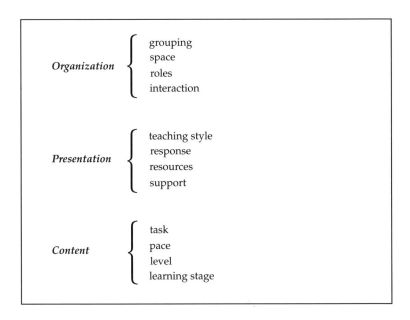

Figure 5.2 Differentiation strategies (adapted from Bailey 2001).

Organizational strategies

Differentiation by grouping
There are numerous ways of grouping children for a particular task, for example:

- ability;
- gender;
- friendship;
- random.

Judith Rink (1993: 70) suggests that 'grouping is a powerful tool that a teacher can use to influence the learning process', and it is worth giving some thought about the most suitable form of grouping for the different activities being planned.

A great deal depends on the children, the intended outcomes from the task, and the type of activity taking place. Older children, when given the choice, will often group themselves in generally similar ability groups in physical education lessons. Younger children do not seem to have such a well-developed sense of their and others' abilities, so tend to prefer working with their friends. There may be times when the teacher wishes to push on the most able pupils, and this may be done best by putting these children into one group for some activities. There will be other times when it really does not matter whether children are working with those of similar ability or not. Sometimes it may be worthwhile encouraging boys and girls to work together. At other times, this may not be appropriate (for example, according to Sheila Scraton (1993), unless the teacher positively intervenes, the boys can dominate lessons, both verbally and physically, take up more of the teacher's time, and push the girls to the margins).

The size of the group is also an important consideration. Generally speaking, the smaller the group size, the easier it is for pupils to deal with the intellectual challenges presented to them: larger groups mean more choices and more decisions, and the potential for more mistakes. It is often useful to allow children to work alone or in pairs when they are first introduced to an activity, as this can put them under less pressure and give them more space to explore and experiment.

Differentiation by space
Changing the amount of space allowed for the performance of a task can make it easier or more difficult. Some children with special needs, such as those using a wheelchair or with crutches, may need more space to turn, change direction or simply for safety. Increasing the available space to play a game, for example, can give the players more time to think and act, and decreasing it can make the game more challenging and quicker. It is also possible to divide the area up, and to restrict some players' movements around the playing area. Specifying zones in which children must work

makes decision making easier, and stops a small number of children from dominating the activity.

Different ways of dividing up an area are shown in Figure 5.3.

Differentiation by roles
Many activities in PE sessions involve a number of different roles. For example, a game of rounders might involve a pitcher, a batter, some fielders and a backstop. It might also include referee, captains and scorers. Ideally, all of the children will experience each of the roles, in order to build up a complete understanding of the activity. However, those who are injured, or are otherwise unable to take part in all of the physical aspects of the lesson can still develop their knowledge and understanding by focusing on the other roles.

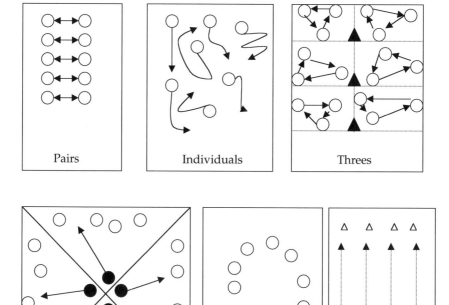

Figure 5.3 Organization of groups and space.

Differentiation by interaction

Physical education tasks can be cooperative, competitive or individual. In other words, children can play with others, against others or by themselves. Each of these formats has its uses, and each has its limitations. When a physical skill is being learned, it may be worthwhile to allow young learners initially to practise without the extra pressures presented by other children (individual). Once the basic skill has been learned with some degree of consistency, they may be organized to work with another child or small group (cooperation), and later the skill might be tested in a fun game playing against other children (competition).

Some children with behaviour problems can find competitive activities particularly stressful, and this can trigger overexcitement or misbehaviour. Of course, cooperative tasks can also present a challenge, especially to the very young or children with an autistic spectrum disorder, and therefore may need gradual introduction to working successfully with others. Non-teaching assistants can be invaluable in supporting children learn these vital skills, such as by joining in and modelling suitable behaviour or by pointing out cues to appropriate action.

Almost any activity in PE can be organized in terms of cooperative, competitive or individual forms of interaction. Take, as an example, the skill of rolling a large ball:

- Individual activity: A learner looks around the area for a space, rolls the ball into that space, follows and picks it up. Looks for a space, and carries on rolling and picking it up.
- Co-operative activity: The class sits in a large circle. One child is given the ball, and asked to call out the name of someone on the other side of the circle, and then roll the ball straight to the chosen person, who then calls out someone else's name and rolls to them.
- Competitive activity: One child stands in front of a 'goal' (two cones placed a metre apart). Another child tries to roll the ball into the goal. The 'defender' tries to protect the goal, and then rolls the ball back to the attacker for another try.

Presentational strategies

Differentiation by teaching style

One method of adapting the way in which teaching is presented to children is by using a variety of styles, and the most popular among physical educators is that of Mosston and Ashworth (1986). They suggest that there is a *spectrum* of teaching styles based around the central importance of *decision making* in the teaching process. The spectrum represents two key themes: a direct, teacher-led approach, juxtaposed with an indirect, child-centred style where the teacher acts as facilitator (Macfadyen and Bailey 2002). The specific styles that make up the spectrum are outlined in Table 5.1.

Different learning outcomes may demand different teaching styles. If the teacher or early years practitioner is introducing a specific skill, especially if there is a safety principle involved, then a direct style may be most appropriate. On the other hand, if the adult wants the learners to reflect on their performances or to consider a range of possible courses of actions, then more indirect styles may be more relevant.

Table 5.1   The spectrum of teaching styles

Command style	All decisions made by the teacher who usually breaks down the skill, step by step. The group responds uniformly to specific instructions.
Practice	Similar to command as the teacher makes most of the decisions and provides the feedback to learners; the children can make some organizational decisions during the lesson.
Reciprocal	Planned by the teacher, who provides clear criteria (e.g. on teaching cards) for the children, who take greater responsibility by teaching each other in pairs/small groups.
Self-check	Planned by the teacher who provides performance criteria task cards, that are used by the children to facilitate and assess their progress of learning.
Inclusion	Similar to self-check but emphasis is on individuals, who start the task at a performance level geared to their own ability; the teacher therefore provides a range of 'entry points'.
Guided discovery	Intended learning outcomes are planned by the teacher, who presents a series of questions that lead the learners to 'discover' the answer.
Problem solving	Emphasis is on children's abilities to create, so the teacher sets a question/problem that has a number of acceptable solutions.
Individual programme	The teacher suggests the subject matter but the children plan and design the programme, seeking the teacher's help when required.
Learner initiated	With the teacher's approval, the children assume almost all responsibility for selecting, planning and designing the subject matter, which is then submitted to the teacher for evaluation.
Self-teaching	Full responsibility for learning is taken by the children.

Differentiation by response
Children can show their knowledge or skills in a wide variety of ways. Within the context of a physical education activity, this might be by demonstrating, explaining, answering questions, writing or drawing, and individually, with a partner or as part of a group. The distinctively public nature of the subject means that some children may feel uncomfortable demonstrating their skills, but may be perfectly happy to explain their ideas to the teacher. Others may be happier showing their progress through performing as part of a group than as an individual. As in so much else, good teaching requires sensitivity to individual difference and needs.

Differentiation by resources
Consider the following example. A group is playing a simple bat and ball game, in which one player throws a small ball to a partner, who uses a bat to try to hit the ball into space, run around a marker and back to the starting position before the rest of the players return the ball to the thrower. It becomes clear, through observation, that some children are struggling with the task, and are hardly managing to hit the ball at all. What can you do? One approach would be to change the resources being used. In the example given here, there are at least three changes to resources that a teacher might make. First, the player can be given a bat with a larger striking area. Second, a different ball can be used; perhaps a larger or lighter ball. Third, instead of receiving a thrown ball (which even professional cricketers and baseball players find a problem), the ball can be struck from a stand. As the player's ability or confidence increases, the resources can be adapted to increase the level of difficulty and challenge.

There are countless other ways in which resources can be adapted or changed to better meet the needs of learners, such as offering 'water wings' to novice swimmers, replacing balls with bean bags to aid throwing and catching, or using different tempos of music for dance. The decision to change resources need not lie only with the adult. Providing a variety of sizes, shapes and weights of equipment for an activity allows learners to pick and choose the most suitable resources for them, and, in doing so, engage intellectually, as well as physically, in the session.

Differentiation by support
Teachers can choose to use their time, and that of any other adult helpers available in different ways. Some times extra help is needed for specific activities, as when giving support in gymnastics. At other times, individuals or groups may benefit from a little extra attention from the teacher, or from focused observation. Some children with special needs may have

a designated non-teaching assistant to support them, and it is important to plan for these assistants' time, as well as their own.

Content-related strategies

Differentiation by task
One of the most common forms of differentiation is to plan different tasks (or different versions of the same task) to match children's abilities or needs. Within the context of a gymnastic activity, for example, children might be asked to demonstrate different balances. Some may try to hold any body shape, whilst others might be encouraged to balance on only two parts of the body, only large surfaces, only small surfaces, or both hands and feet. All of the children are engaged in balancing, but they are all experiencing slightly different versions of the same task.

Differentiation by pace
Children may progress through the planned activities at different rates. This may be a result of physical fitness, motivation or understanding. One way to plan for differentiation by pace is to provide workcards for the different tasks in an activity, and children progress through these cards at their own speed. Another way is to group children according to ability, and to extend the challenges presented to the more able or fitter groups, and give more time for the slower or less able groups.

Differentiation by level
Learners can work at tasks at different levels of challenge. For example, running activities can be completed at different speeds, gymnastics skills can be performed with different levels of difficulty and games can be played with different sizes of teams. In each case, the differentiation takes place through the level of challenge presented to learners.

Differentiation by learning stage
In Chapter 3, it was suggested that children pass through a series of stages, as they acquire and develop their movement skills. This pattern seems fairly consistent across a wide range of skills and learners of different ages, and there are specific teaching methods and strategies that are likely to be most effective in supporting children at different stages of learning (see Figure 5.4).

Refinement   practice; self- and peer-analysis of skills

Selection   application of skills in specific contexts

Combination   demonstration and explanation; practice with variety of
             equipment and contexts

Discovery   guided discovery; problem-solving challenges

Exploration   play; time and opportunity to experiment

Figure 5.4   Teaching methods related to stages of learning a movement skill.

Organizing the activity

Inclusive practices in physical education do not demand that all learners participate at all times alongside their peers. Rather, it suggests that children should be included in lessons as far as is possible and in their best interests. The keys here are flexibility of approach and sensitivity to the needs and wishes of the individual, and the best ways to inform both of these points are to observe what is taking place, discuss the situation with the individual, and listen.

There is no one 'best way' to teach children; so much depends on the needs of the learners and the specific context of the activity. One approach is the 'Inclusion Spectrum' (adapted from Black and Haskins 1996). According to this model, there are five main methods of organizing and delivering an activity: separate, adapted, parallel, modified and inclusive, and these are represented in Figure 5.5.

Inclusive activities are those in which everyone in the group is included, without adapting or modifying the activity. Depending on the range of abilities, this might involve the whole group joining in a simple clapping game at the start of a dance activity, or stretching in preparation for a gymnastics session.

Modified activities involve the sorts of differentiation strategies discussed in

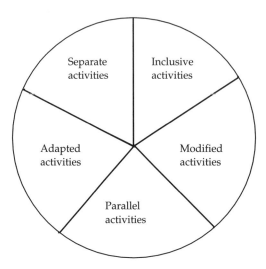

Figure 5.5 The Inclusion Spectrum.

the previous section – differentiated rules, space, equipment, roles and so on. Whilst there is differentiated or modified performance for children with different needs, all work together on the same general task in the same area.

Parallel activities are those in which children of different abilities are grouped together, and participate in their own way, but in the same task. For example, wheelchair users and other children might form two groups for games of volleyball.

Adapted activities, or 'reverse integration', occur when all pupils take part in adapted tasks, or tasks that are designed with specific groups in mind, such as children with physical disabilities. For example, all pupils might play Bocchia (an aiming game, rather like French Petanque or Bowls) together. This approach has the dual advantage of introducing the class to new and exciting games, but also an activity with which the disabled child is likely to have more experience than the rest of the group (a very rare experience in physical education activities).

Separate activities take place when a specific group of children practise an activity on their own. This might be in preparation for a competition, or for a movement assessment.

The approaches used will depend on a range of factors, such as the task being undertaken, the ability level and range of the children, and the learning objectives of the activity. Whatever the approach adopted, it is important not to be dogmatic about its use. There is no correct way, in absolute terms, only more or less appropriate ways in specific situations. The goal of inclusive practice is to meet the needs of all the children. A flexible use of a range of strategies increases the likelihood that they will be challenged and motivated, and that none will feel excluded from physical education.

Conclusion

Good teaching is good teaching, and teachers need to recognize the distinctive and essential contribution that physical education can make to *all* children, whatever their ability. The virtue of the language and the concept of inclusion, rather than special educational needs, is that it reminds us that teaching children with difficulties or disabilities is essentially the same task as any other sort of teaching, and draws on the same sorts of skills. It might be claimed that physical activity is an especially important, although often overlooked, feature of inclusive practice. In the words of Jerome Bruner (1983: 121), movement, activity and play represent the 'culture of childhood'. Children seem to have an instinctive need to experience this culture, and it is best experienced in the company of other children.

6

Physical activity and children's health

Regular physical activity is an important part of a healthy lifestyle.

Introduction

There is little doubt that regular physical activity is an important part of a healthy lifestyle. Physical activity can promote greater energy and vitality, it can increase fitness to carry out daily tasks and can also combat a variety of illnesses and conditions. Unfortunately, it is becoming increasingly evident that many of us are not active enough, and that numerous disturbing health risks can result from our sedentary behaviours. For example, recent evidence has highlighted an alarming increase in obesity in British children (Chinn and Rona 2001), and there is concern that this reduces overall quality of life and increases the risk of ill health and premature death in later life.

Few parents of young children worry about their offspring's low levels of activity. On the contrary, infants make up the most physically active part of the population. Children love to move. They seem to have never-ending supplies of energy, and revel in trying out new physical skills, practising established ones and testing their limits in ever more ingenious ways. The psychologist, Jerome Bruner (1983: 121) suggested that action, play and movement make up the 'culture of childhood', and others (Rowland 1998; Bailey 1999a) have hinted at an activity 'drive', that pushes young children to look for and capitalize on opportunities for movement and physically active play. Despite this, however, some authorities have started to express concerns that children's opportunities for physical activity are being threatened by changes to their physical and social environments, and that some children are experiencing uncharacteristically inactive lifestyles from a disturbingly early age.

Health and physical activity

The health benefits of regular physical activity for adults is very well established. Regular participation in such activities is associated with a longer and better quality of life, reduced risks of a variety of diseases and many psychological and emotional benefits (Sallis and Owen 1999). There is also a large body of literature showing that inactivity is one of the most significant causes of death, disability and reduced quality of life in the Western world (US Department of Health and Human Services 1996).

Summarizing research evidence on the positive effects of physical activity for children and young people, Stuart Biddle and his colleagues (1998: 4–5) highlight the following benefits:

- psychological well-being;
- self-esteem;

- moral and social development;
- overweight and obesity;
- chronic disease risk factors;
- physical activity 'tracking'.

These factors set the context for the subsequent discussion, and are worth considering in more detail.

Psychological well-being and self-esteem

These are important, but often overlooked, aspects of children's health. In recent years, there has been evidence of disturbingly high rates of mental ill health among adolescents and even younger children, ranging from low self-esteem, anxiety and depression to eating disorders, substance abuse and suicide (Sallis and Owen 1999). There is fairly consistent evidence that regular activity can have a positive effect on the psychological well-being of children and young people. Reviewing the literature in the area, Mutrie and Parfitt (1998) conclude that physical activity is positively associated with good mental health. The case is particularly strong in the case of children's self-esteem, especially so in disadvantaged groups, such as those with learning difficulties or initially low self-esteem. Other associations with regular activity that have been reported include reduced stress, anxiety and depression, all of which lend support to Sallis and Owen's (1999: 51) claim that 'physical activity improves psychological health in young people'.

Moral and social development

The view that participation in physical activities can contribute to children's moral and social development has a long history. Indeed, politicians frequently cite it as one of the main justifications for the inclusion of physical education and sport in the school curriculum (e.g. Department of National Heritage 1995). The evidence is less certain than the politicians: whilst there are some studies that claim that physical activities can enhance social and moral development, there are others that suggest participation can actually damage such development. Evaluating the case, Bailey (2000b) concluded that a great deal depends on the way in which activities are presented to children, and that teachers or parents can make a great contribution to the values and lessons that children pick up from their participation in physical activities.

Overweight and obesity

There seems to be a general trend towards increased obesity, or over-fatness, across the population, and it has been predicted that by 2005, 18 per cent of men and 24 per cent of women in the United Kingdom will be obese (Department for Health 1995). This growing problem is reflected in an increase in overweight and obesity in children, and by the time they leave primary school, as many as 21 per cent of boys and 14 per cent of girls are approaching a concerning level of fatness. Evidence suggests that the infant years represent a 'critical period' for the development of lifelong obesity (Whitaker *et al.* 1998). Obesity that begins during this period appears to increase the risk of persistent obesity and the associated risks like coronary heart disease and diabetes (Freedman *et al.* 2001).

Regular exercise represents an important weapon in the battle against childhood obesity especially when combined with dietary changes. It also seems to be the case that the younger the child at the start of regular physical activity, the more marked and longer lasting are the results (Armstrong and Welsman 1997). So, the early years are vital in the battle against obesity.

Chronic disease risk factors

Physical activity may influence the physical health of children in two ways. First, it could affect the causes of disease during childhood. Second, it could reduce the risk for chronic diseases in later life (Sallis and Owen 1999). Evidence is starting to appear suggesting a favourable relationship between physical activity and a host of factors affecting children's physical health, including diabetes, blood pressure, the ability to use fat for energy and bone health (Bailey 1999a). Interestingly, it also seems to be the case that a number of 'adult' conditions, such as osteoporosis (brittle bones) and coronary heart disease, have their origins in childhood, and can be aided, in part, by regular physical activity in the early years.

Physical activity 'tracking'

It seems common sense to suppose that instilling good exercise habits early in life will increase the likelihood of a physically active lifestyle later on. Research has yet to supply strong evidence that this is really the case. The strongest link is between childhood and adolescent levels of activity, whilst the relationship is less clear as individuals progress to adulthood (Malina 1996). Nevertheless, until more results are in, it seems sensible to work on the assumption that teaching good exercise habits to young children will have some positive effects later in life.

Children's levels of physical activity

It seems slightly absurd to question whether children are sufficiently physically active to be healthy. After all, they make up the most physically
active part of the population, and the suggestion has been made that they
are 'naturally' active, and proactively seek out opportunities to move and
play. If children are not active enough, what chance for the rest of us?

Disturbingly, some writers have started to raise concerns regarding the
levels of health among certain groups of children, and physical inactivity
has been identified as a possible contributory cause. Hypokinetic diseases
(diseases related to physical inactivity) are being witnessed in increasingly
younger children, and these diseases include coronary heart disease,
obesity, high blood pressure, high blood cholesterol, diabetes, back pain,
stress and depression (Biddle and Biddle 1989). One study in Northern
Ireland (Boreham et al. 1992) found that over 69 per cent of 12-year-olds
had at least one modifiable risk factor for coronary heart disease, with 14
per cent exhibiting three or more risk factors. In a review of the findings
related to the fatty build up on the walls of the arteries, one researcher
wrote: 'we can say with certainty that coronary atherosclerosis has its origins in childhood, at least by the age of 10 and possibly earlier' (McGill
1984: 451).

Whether or not these disturbing findings can be laid at the door of
physical inactivity is a debated point (Riddoch 1998). Certainly, some
studies make uncomfortable reading. For example, Baranowski and his
colleagues (1987) observed 24 7- to 10-year-olds for over 9 hours on each
of two days. Using '20 minutes in which rapid trunk movement through
space was maintained without stopping' as their criterion for recording
aerobic physical activity, they did not record one single incident in a total
of 432 hours of observations. Another study (Bailey et al. 1995) analysed
the level and tempo of activity of 6- to 10-year-olds over nine periods of
4 hours' observation, carried out both during the school day and at
weekends or holidays. The study found that the children spent the
majority of their time engaged in activities of low intensity, and over an
average period of 12 hours, spent 22 minutes doing high intensity
physical activities. No period of activity lasting 10 minutes or more was
recorded, and almost all of the instances of physical activity lasted less
than 15 seconds.

Other studies have given greater reason to be optimistic (e.g. Sleep and
Warburton 1996), but even these reveal that there are many children who
are living habitually sedentary lives. The following warning is stark, but
may be accurate: 'For lack of exercise, we are bringing up a generation of
children less healthy than it could be, and many of whom are likely to be

at high risk in later life of serious disease and shortened life expectancy'
(Morris, in Sports Council 1988: 3).

How active do children need to be?

> Children are not simply small adults. Indeed, they differ from adults
> qualitatively as well as quantitatively, when it comes to exercise
> physiology.
>
> (Sharp 1991: 70)

The claim that children are not just miniature adults has been repeated so
often in post-Piagetian times that it has become something of a cliché.
However, it is important not to ignore the central importance of the statement in any area concerning children, their development and education.
Paediatric exercise physiology, the branch of science concerned with
children's responses to physical activity, is still in its infancy, and a clear
picture of the type and amount of exercise that children require is still in
the process of emerging.

Charles Corbin and his colleagues have suggested that there were three
main stages in the evolution of our understanding of appropriate physical
activity levels for children and young people (Corbin *et al.* 1994; see Table
6.1). For many years, medics and scientists cautioned that children were
not able to perform vigorous physical activities. The main reason they normally gave, which has subsequently proved to be incorrect, was that the
child's heart and blood vessels developed at different rates, and, therefore,
there was a serious danger of damage to the heart if it underwent strenuous exertion. As recently as the late 1960s, textbooks were making claims
such as: 'too strenuous exercise may cause an enlargement of the heart
and result in valvular disease' (Hurlock's *Adolescent Development*, cited

Table 6.1 The evolution of our understanding of appropriate physical activity
levels for children

Stage 1	The child as incapable	Children are not able to perform vigorous exercise, and so should not be taxed too hard or for too long
Stage 2	The child as a mini-adult	The activity guidance for children is essentially the same as that for adults
Stage 3	The child as a child	Child-specific guidance, that acknowledges children's different physical and psychological characteristics, is required

in Corbin *et al.* 1994: 1). A result of this sort of guidance was that many children were excluded from certain forms of sport and physical activity, for fear of overstraining their hearts.

Over time, a body of evidence started to build up indicating that there was no such imbalance between the proportions of children's hearts and blood vessels and that the very foundations of the view that children were incapable of vigorous activity was invalid. So, how much physical activity should children experience?

With limited child-specific evidence to turn to, most physical activity recommendations for children were broadly based on those for adults (Rowland 1985). Since the start of America's fitness boom in the late 1960s and early 1970s, and particularly with the emergence of jogging and aerobic dance as staples of healthy adult lifestyles, a model became increasingly popular which might be called the exercise prescription model (Corbin *et al.* 1994). This model (outlined in Table 6.2) served as the basis for the great majority of health and fitness programmes offered to adults (indeed, you can still see guidance like this in fitness clubs around the country). Traditionally, the exercise prescription model uses the mnemonic FITT to summarize its details, which stands for the Frequency, Intensity, Time and Type of the activity to be undertaken.

There is much to be said in favour of this approach for busy people, with limited amounts of time, since it offers a quick and efficient dose of activity likely to bring about health benefits for any adult able to follow the plan. The trouble is that many adults find it difficult to stick to such a strict regime, as do almost all children (Riddoch 1998).

There are at least two main points of difficulty with the exercise prescription model for children. First, some studies have raised doubts over the central importance of intensity for healthy activity in children. More and more authorities are now suggesting that moderate levels of physical activity can bring about significant health benefits, especially for the relatively unfit (Blair *et al.* 1992). It is also worth pointing out that children rarely manage to sustain *any* level of intensity. Rather, their activity is

Table 6.2 Standard exercise prescription model

Frequency	How often?	At least three times per week
Intensity	How hard?	Moderate to vigorous (140 heart beats per minute, and higher)
Time	How long?	20–30 minutes
Type	What?	Jogging, swimming, aerobic dance – exercises that raise the heart rate to an appropriate level, and maintain it at that level for a block of time

characterized by extreme fluctuations – one moment they are racing at top speed, then they are slowing, then stopping for a chat, then trotting, then racing again. Even in laboratory conditions, it is very difficult to ensure that children, especially younger children, move at a consistent pace. One questions the usefulness of an exercise model to which it is almost impossible to adhere!

Second, exercise scientists have questioned whether the emphasis placed on the duration and frequency of activity is necessary. Whilst blocks of continuous activity may be useful and an effective way for adults to improve their physical *fitness* (for example, in preparation for sports performance), the overall amount of energy expended may be more significant for *health* benefits (Riddoch 1998). In other words, rather than encouraging children to endure blocks of relatively intense activity, we should focus on facilitating an accumulation of activity of varying intensities over the day.

During the 1990s, there has been a gradual change in emphasis regarding the type and amount of physical activity which it is suggested are necessary for children to achieve and maintain optimal health. At the heart of this change has been a recognition of the full significance of the differences between children and adults in terms of exercise and activity. As Craig Sharp's quotation at the start of this section stresses, children are not miniature adults, and a failure to recognize this fact presents a fatal flaw in any model of children's physical activity (see Table 6.3).

Adult-derived models are destined to fail to address the specific needs and characteristics of young children. One example of a model that aims to correct previous misconceptions of children's exercise is the Children's Lifetime Physical Activity Model (Corbin *et al*. 1994; see also Riddoch 1998; Bailey 1999a). Following evidence that moderate physical activity is beneficial in the development of children's health, and that distinctive motivational factors are vitally important if children are going to continue to participate in physical activities as they grow up, the adapted model suggests that children should be given opportunities and support to be physically active on a number of occasions everyday, of varying intensities and durations. This approach proposes the full range of activities, including games, walking, cycling and skill learning (such as in school physical education lessons). Table 6.4 summarizes an activity model based on this evidence.

It is worth noting here that models of this sort suggest a model of activity with great similarity to children's natural physical play. Play may well be the most natural way for children to stay active (Bailey 1999a). It may also be the best way for them to get fit and healthy:

It is an attractive and plausible thought that the optimal level of physical activity for humans may be, in reality, a full day's play as a child, and a full day's labour as an adult. There are powerful influences to restrict both of these, but maybe these are the activity goals, or at least an activity equivalent, for which children and adults should strive.

(Riddoch 1998: 37)

Table 6.3　Some characteristics of children's responses to physical activity and their implications

Children's responses to physical activity	Implications
Children love to move and be physically active	They will be active if given the opportunity and encouragement to do so
Children are wasteful of energy: they tire more easily, and use up relatively large amounts of oxygen	They should avoid prolonged high intensity activity, in favour of activity of varying intensity, with opportunities for rest periods
Children recover from exercise more quickly than adults	They are well-suited to intermittent types of activity, as are often seen in playground games
Children are poor perceivers of effort in exercise	Adult-type 'training' programmes may be inappropriate; varied tasks that emphasize fun and participation should be the rule
Children of different genders, ages, abilities and levels of maturation may be attracted to different types of activity	Provide a variety of activity opportunities; do not emphasize one form as 'better' or more valued than the others

Table 6.4　Adapted physical activity model for children

Frequency	How often?	Every day, with frequent bouts of activity during each day
Intensity	How hard?	Varying intensities – low-moderate-vigorous, with frequent rest periods as needed by the child
Time	How long?	Length of bouts less important than the accumulation of 30–60 minutes of moderate activity
Type	What?	Physical play (chasing, rough-and-tumble, climbing, etc.), walking to and from nursery/playgroup/ school, sports and games, PE lessons, household physical tasks

Children's participation in physical activity

Physical activity is a central feature of children's lives. It makes an essential contribution to their physical, psychological and social well-being. More important still, perhaps, is that it constitutes what Bruner (1983) termed the 'culture of childhood'. It is often through movement and physically active play that children learn about themselves, about their peers and family, and about the relationship between them. It is through movement and activity that children first play and communicate. Movement creates the context in which children learn about their world.

It is worthwhile considering for a while the factors associated with children's physical activity; those things that facilitate or encourage activity, and those things that prevent or restrict it. There is a wide range of theories from psychology and sociology aiming to explain young people's acquisition and development of behaviours and attitudes. Most are premised on a recognition that a great deal of human activity is of a social nature (Wold and Hendry 1998). Whilst it is almost certainly the case that a great deal of the very earliest forms of physical activity are expressions of some sort of internal drive to move, such as the so-called 'rhythmic stereotypes' of young infants (Pellegrini and Smith 1998), the vast majority of actions strongly reflect specific cultural or social patterns.

Television and other electronic media have often been blamed for declining activity levels in young people. The average child in the United Kingdom spends about 20 hours a week watching television (Central Statistical Office 1994). This need not be a detrimental factor, since the mass media has potential for promoting certain behaviours, and they could easily be employed to encourage lifelong physical activity as much as they seem to promote the sedentary enjoyment of trivia and consumption. In practice, when the media do portray physical activities, it is usually élite competitive sports. It is conceivable that watching élite sports may result in the development of more positive attitudes and an increase in activity levels (Hofstetter *et al*. 1995), as if watching David Beckham or Denise Lewis inspires young spectators to emulate their heroes. However, it is also possible that television's portrayal of high level sports players may have the opposite effect, by presenting images that are simply unachievable for the vast majority of observers, and hence demotivate them from taking up the activity (Wold and Hendry 1998). It may also be the case that the media acts as a barrier to activity by its implicit message of sport as passively consumed entertainment (Sallis 1993). Research into this area is somewhat limited. It is common sense to assume that increased television viewing will reduce levels of physical activity, since time spent watching *Grandstand* or *Popstars* is time that children are not being active.

Surprisingly, some studies have shown that this may not be the case, especially among 3- to 8-year-olds (DuRant *et al.* 1994).

Changing transport patterns suggest another factor that seems to negatively affect children's levels of physical activity. For example, between 1975 and 1991, there was a doubling of the proportion of children taking car journeys to school (Central Statistical Office 1994). This relates, to some extent, to parents' increased fears regarding children's safety. Many parents have weighed the benefits of walking to school, shops and so on against the perceived costs to personal safety, such as hazardous road conditions and threats to personal safety by assault (Scott *et al.* 2000). This has resulted in many deciding in favour of car travel, despite the possible consequences to long-term health.

Mayer Hillman, of the Policy Studies Institute, has analysed trends of 'independent mobility', that is, children's freedom to take part in outdoor activities, and found that there had been a decline with time. His survey of 7- to 11-year-olds found a significant reduction in independent mobility between 1971 and 1990. For example, only one-quarter of that group were allowed to use their cycles on the road in 1990, compared with two-thirds in 1971, and four times as many children in 1990 were driven to school than in 1971. A further dimension of Hillman's research related to gender. Boys were allowed far more independent mobility than girls in all areas studied, such as access to leisure places, walking unaccompanied to school and cycling on roads (Hillman 1993). Nevertheless, young children still do take part in out-of-doors play and sporting activities, especially if opportunities are made available. Significantly, the more places that are available in which children can play, the more they do play.

These are, of course, only a few of the factors that may influence children's participation in physical activities. There are numerous others. Sallis (1995) offered a neat summary of the types of factors in terms of 'personal' and 'environmental' dimensions. A simplified outline of this model is presented in Table 6.5.

A number of factors related to the biological make-up of the individual have been found to influence children's participation in physical activities. Evidence identifies age and gender as particularly important variables. Both boys and girls reduce the amount of activity they do as they get older, with some studies suggesting a 50–75 per cent reduction in levels of physical activity between 6 and 18 years of age (Rowland 1990). However, the rate of decline is especially great for girls – showing about 2.5 per cent greater decline than boys between 6 and 17 years (Armstrong and Welsman 1997). The pattern of activity levels is portrayed in simplified form in Figure 6.1 (based on data reported in Rowland 1990; Pellegrini and Smith 1998).

Table 6.5 Factors influencing children's participation in physical activity (adapted from Sallis 1995)

Personal factors		Environmental factors	
Biological	*Psychological*	*Social*	*Physical*
Age	Motivation	Parents	Weather
Gender	Perceived barriers	Peers	Season
Obesity	Perceived competence	Practitioners/ Teachers/School PE	Access
Fitness Levels	Beliefs	Culture	Type of activity
Heredity	Attitudes	Media	Way activity is promoted

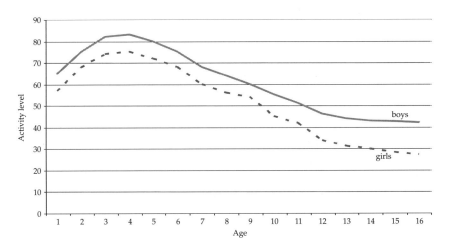

Figure 6.1 Physical activity during childhood and adolescence.

It is often difficult to interpret data on psychological factors: studies are frequently based on discrete theoretical perspectives, making comparison and accumulation of evidence difficult; the problem becomes especially severe when the subject is a young child, since standard methodological tools, like self-reporting, questionnaires and interviews, might yield imprecise or dubious results. Nevertheless, certain patterns have begun to emerge. Young children readily accept that physical activities are important for health and fitness, but this does not necessarily lead them to take part in such activities. Infants and even older children seem to have an innate sense of their own immortality, and long-term health benefits lack immediate appeal. More successful motivating factors seem to be fun and enjoyment (Petlickoff 1992), and children's interpretation of activities as fun stem from such things as the excitement of the game, improving their skills, a sense of accomplishment, a positive perception of their own performance and the amount of effort required (Health Education Authority 1997).

Children's perceived barriers to participation are of particular importance, as they give clues both to reasons for declining levels of activity, and to strategies for addressing this decline. Most studies have focused on adolescents, and one might guess a whole host of additional obstacles raised by parents and young children, especially in terms of concerns about risk and personal safety. Scott and her colleagues, for example, interviewed parents and children and found that strangers, drugs and traffic were identified as the main risks to children by both groups (Scott *et al.* 2000). Other possible perceived barriers include lack of success, parental pressure, expense, limited awareness of the available opportunities and bad weather (Sports Council 1993).

Social factors, like parents, teachers and peers, play an important role in influencing children's attitudes and behaviour. Whilst adolescents are especially guided by friends, younger children are more influenced by parents, other family members and teachers (Sallis 1995). Toddlers seem to be especially open to parental encouragement to be physically active, whilst older children respond more directly to role modelling, so there is a very strong link between parents' and their primary-aged children's levels of activity: the more active the parents, the more active the children (Klesges *et al.* 1986). One interesting study found that children with physically active mothers were twice as likely to be active as children of inactive mothers. If both parents were physically active, children were six times as likely to be active (Moore *et al.* 1991).

Promoting health and physical activity: some conclusions and recommendations

> Physical Education makes me feel as if I could fly away!
> (Leeds Primary School pupil, quoted in Talbot 1999)

This chapter has identified a number of causes for concern with regard to children's current levels of health and physical activity. Whilst many, probably most, children continue to live active, healthy lives, an increasing number seem to experience steady reductions in opportunities for physically active play and transport.

A positive feature of the discussion, to which we must return whenever the matter is raised, is that children, given half a chance, love to move and play. This explains the persistent popularity of physical education lessons for primary-aged children, and the barely restrained eagerness with which they embark on races, rough and tumble and playground games. Opportunities for physical activity need not be expensive; indeed, it need not cost anything at all. Children require very few elements to play: they need a place to play; they sometimes need things with which to play, of which the most flexible, exciting and effective is other children; and they need time to play.

The encouragement of physical activity is best started early, building on children's natural inquisitiveness and drive to move. In order to succeed, we need to remember that children are not miniature adults. Their bodies and minds respond very differently than those of adults. The physical differences are discussed earlier in this chapter, but it is worthwhile stressing here an important psychological difference. The typical health and fitness messages that may motivate or alarm adults, such as threats of obesity or shortened life expectancy, mean little to young children living in the present moment, with a sneaking suspicion that they are immortal! In order to succeed, any programme hoping to get and keep children active should be appealing, enjoyable and social (Harris and Elbourn 1997). It should also be normal, habitual and as natural a part of a child's day as possible, if it is to become and remain a central feature of a child's life. In summary, children need:

- a place to play;
- things or people to play with;
- time to play.

The activity should be:

- appealing;
- enjoyable;
- social;
- normal;
- habitual;
- natural.

7

The physically educated child

The period from birth to six years lays the foundations for future movement and for a physically literate population.

Introduction

The approach advocated in this book is that physical education is for life and that a variety of meaningful and empowering movement experiences should be made available for every child. A major aim of physical education is to make available to children experiences that contribute to this aim and in so doing improve the quality of life for every child. In their formative years, all children should be helped to develop competence that leads to them having confidence in their physical abilities. Alongside this must be an eagerness to take part regularly in some form of physical activity as children view it as an enjoyable and important part of their lives.

Developmentally appropriate movement experiences

Objectives in physical education that are broad and general are not helpful for those parents, teachers and carers seeking to provide movement experiences that are meaningful and relevant for each child. It is insufficient to simply expose children to certain physical activities and assume a host of different outcomes will ensue automatically. What are needed are activities that emphasize both children's learning and adult support, teaching and encouragement. In this way children may be helped to discover and find true meaning in and through movement. The vision here is for a programme of physical movement experiences for every child, with each having the opportunity to find success at their own individual level.

Movement experiences in this vision go much further than mere performance of movement tasks, repetition of motor skills or participation in fitness activities. The essence of this approach is on a conceptual framework based on process. Emphasis on product (i.e. goals and outcome), based on traditional activities and methods of instruction, has resulted in uninformed learning and lack of understanding on the part of children. In this often technique-led approach we see instruction in specific drills and skills and an emphasis on organization of groups of children rather than on their learning. It is about rigid performance with little creativity and often mindless participation in activities with low cognitive or social involvement.

Emphasis on the process of developing movement skills and knowledge, in contrast, has its focus on the children and their learning. Children's abilities, needs and interests are specific to them, and learning experiences need to be designed with this in mind. This approach appreciates and celebrates the relationship between movement and all other areas of learning. It is not bound by adult labels such as 'gymnastics', 'games' or 'dance', but embraces movement wherever it happens – at home, in the park, on the beach, at schools, nurseries and playgroups, indoors and outdoors. Such an approach makes full use of inspiring movement activities that stimulate children's thinking, foster enjoyment and success, and promote their desire to be involved in physical activity wherever the context for learning takes place. It involves children developing skills to solve physical challenges, learning from and teaching others, understanding and being able to talk about movement, and developing a range of motor skills that form the foundation for a lifetime in movement.

The concept of a physically educated child

Society is in a time of rapid change. As educators we need to respond to this change and programmes of learning need to enable children to live in today's world but also prepare them to live in tomorrow's. What is certain is that in tomorrow's world there will be new opportunities and possibilities. What then do we consider to be the child who has this preparation? Look for the children who enjoy the thrill of moving. They can move in any context and transfer skills from one context to another. Their movements are efficient and exact or graceful and flowing when required. There is a quality in their actions which is instantly recognizable. They are eager for new movement experiences, independent, but also cooperative, attentive to learn new skills and improve existing ones. They are children who are highly motivated, bubbling with life and vitality. We describe such children as being 'physically educated'.

Factors that are associated with the promotion of the physically educated child, according to Maude (2001), are:

- environments, equipment and resources;
- curriculum;
- time.

Environments, equipment and resources

Werner and Burton (1979: 3) remind us that 'active learning requires a physical environment designed for this specific purpose'. To maximize learning opportunities this should include indoor and outdoor facilities in an environment that seeks to stimulate curiosity and a desire to explore and participate. Babies and toddlers require an environment that is safe and clean, with equipment and play materials to meet their specific needs.

Older children will respond to situations that are safe but challenging and will enjoy practising their developing skills with a range of equipment and in different contexts.

Curriculum

The view taken in this book is that physical education places the child at the centre of the learning process. It views physical education in the context of learning and holistic development. Value is given to learning experiences that are designed to promote the social, intellectual, emotional, linguistic as well as physical development of every child. A similar view is taken by Wetton in her advice on establishing an educationally sound physical education curriculum for the Early Years. She states that 'the curriculum should be structured as an integral part of the total school curriculum and should reflect the schools' philosophy about their particular children's needs and the ways in which their own children learn' (Wetton 1988: 1). In its educative role, therefore, a physical education curriculum should challenge all aspects of children's development, initiate them into the sports of our own and others' cultures and provide knowledge and choice about the maintenance of safe and active lifestyles.

Time

For its direct impact on embedding motor skills and knowledge, time may be seen to be the most valued resource of all, and perhaps the scarcest. A number of surveys have reviewed the amount of curriculum time spent on physical education, nationally revealing a steady decline in the time allocated to the subject (NAHT 1999). In their worldwide survey presented to the World Summit on Physical Education, Hardman and Marshall (2001: 32) reported that,

> Physical education has been pushed into a defensive position. It is suffering from decreasing curriculum time allocation, budgetary controls with inadequate financial, material and personnel resources, has low subject status and esteem, and is being ever more marginalised and undervalued by authorities. At best, it seems to occupy a tenuous place in the school curriculum: in many countries, it is not accepted on a par with seemingly superior academic subjects concerned with developing a child's intellect.

Towards physical literacy

The period from birth to 6 years is a formative one, laying the foundation for future movement. In the same way it is also the foundation for a physically literate population. This concept has been used by physical educators for some years and yet a clear definition of what it is remains elusive. The debate centres around questions like, 'What are the capacities needed to be physically literate?' and 'How does the concept affect current and future practice in physical education?' Our view, and the philosophy of physical education expounded in this book, is admirably reflected in the words of Margaret Whitehead (2000: 10):

> the characteristics of a physically literate individual are that the person moves with poise, economy and confidence in a wide variety of physically challenging situations. In addition the individual is perceptive in 'reading' all aspects of the physical environment, anticipating movement needs or possibilities and responding appropriately to these, with intelligence and imagination. Physical literacy requires a holistic engagement that encompasses physical capacities embedded in perception, experience, memory, anticipation and decision making.

Conclusion

To draw our discussion to a close, we finish with a brief statement of our vision of physical education for young children. This statement makes no claims of authority. On the contrary, it aims to cause readers to reflect on their own visions, and to consider the practical ways in which they might come to realize them.

Physically educated children:

1 Enjoy the thrill of moving and taking part in movement activities.
2 Build on a firm foundational base of movement experiences as they grow older.
3 Are involved in some form of physical activity on a daily basis.
4 Experience a wide range of physical events.
5 Appreciate how physical activity provides opportunities for self-expression and communication.
6 Appreciate the role of regular activity in lifelong health and wellness.
7 Are able to choose particular activities based on personal aptitudes and interests.

8 Acquire new physical skills enthusiastically.
9 Observe movement and verbalize what they see.
10 Recognize the requirement to practise regularly to improve movement skills.
11 Enjoy working alone and with others in different forms of physical activity.
12 Have an understanding of safety and risk.
13 Select and use appropriate equipment.
14 Look forward to sessions of play and physical activity.

References

Almond, L. (2000) Physical education and primary schools, in R.P. Bailey and T.M. Macfadyen (eds) *Teaching Physical Education 5–11*. London: Continuum.

Armstrong, N. and Welsman, J. (1997) *Young People and Physical Activity*. Oxford: Oxford University Press.

Arnold, P.J. (1979) *Meaning in Movement, Sport and Physical Education*. London: Heinemann.

Aslin, R.N. (1981) Development of smooth pursuit in human infants, in D.F. Fisher, R.A. Monty and J.W. Senders (eds) *Eye Movements: Cognition and Visual Perception*. Hillsdale, NJ: Erlbaum.

Aslin, R.N. and Dumais, S.T. (1980) Binocular vision in infants: a review and a theoretical position. *Advances in Child Development and Behaviour*, 15: 53–94.

Aslin, R.N. and Salapatek, P. (1975) Saccadic localization of peripheral targets by the very young human infant. *Perception and Psychophysics*, 17: 292–302.

Ayres, A.J. (1978) *Southern California Sensory-Motor Integration Test Manual*. Los Angeles, CA: Western Psychological Corporation.

Bailey, R.P. (1999a) Play, health and physical development, in T. David (ed.) *Young Children Learning*. London: Paul Chapman.

Bailey, R.P. (1999b) Physical education: action, play, movement, in J. Riley and R. Prentice (eds) *The Primary Curriculum 7–11*. London: Paul Chapman.

Bailey, R.P. (2000a) Movement development and the primary school child, in R.P. Bailey and T.M. Macfadyen (eds) *Teaching Physical Education 5–11*. London: Continuum.

Bailey, R.P. (2000b) The value and values of physical education and sport, in R.P. Bailey (ed.) *Teaching Values and Citizenship Across the Curriculum*. London: Kogan Page.

Bailey, R.P. (2001) *Teaching Physical Education: A Handbook for Primary and Secondary Teachers*. London: Kogan Page.

Bailey, R.P. and Robertson, C.R. (2000) Including *all* pupils in primary school physical education, in R.P. Bailey and T.M. Macfadyen (eds) *Teaching Physical Education 5–11*. London: Continuum.

Bailey, R., Olson, J., Pepper, S. *et al.* (1995) The level and tempo of children's physical activities: an observational study. *Medicine and Science in Sports and Exercise*, 27: 1033–41.

Bandura, A. (1969) Social learning theory of identificatory process, in D. Goslin (ed.) *Handbook of Socialization Theory and Research*. Chicago, IL: Rand McNally.

Bandura, A. (1997) *Social Learning Theory*. Englewood Cliffs, NJ: Prentice Hall.

Banks, M.S. and Ginsburg, A.P. (1985) Infant visual preferences: a review and new theoretical treatment. *Advances in Child Development and Behaviour*, 19: 207–46.

Baranowski, T., Tsong, Y., Hooks, P., Cieslik, C. and Nader, P.R. (1987) Aerobic physical activity among third to sixth grade children. *Journal of Developmental and Behavioural Pediatrics*, 8: 203–6.

Barrett, K.R. (1984) The teacher as observer, interpreter, and decision-maker, in B.J. Logsdon, K. Barrett, M. Broer *et al.* (eds) *Physical Education for Children: A Focus on the Teaching Process*. Philadelphia, PA: Lea and Febiger.

Barton L. (1993) Disability, empowerment and physical education, in J. Evans (ed.) *Equality, Education and Physical Education*. London: Falmer.

Bayley, N. (1993) *Bayley Scales of Infant Development*. San Antonio, TX: The Psychological Corporation.

Beashel, P. and Taylor, J. (1996) (eds) *Advanced Studies in Physical Education and Sport*. Surrey: ITP, Nelson.

Beaumont, G. (1997) *Curriculum Bank. Key Stage One Scottish Levels A–B. Physical Education*. Warwickshire: Scholastic Publications.

Bee, H. (2000) *The Developing Child*, 4th edn. Needham Heights, MA: Allyn and Bacon.

Biddle, S. and Biddle, G. (1989) Health-related fitness for the primary school, in A. Williams (ed.) *Issues in Physical Education in the Primary Years*. London: Falmer Press.

Biddle, S., Cavill, N. and Sallis, J. (1998) Policy framework for young people and health-enhancing physical activity, in S. Biddle, J. Sallis and N. Cavill (eds) *Young and Active? Young People and Health-enhancing Physical Activity – Evidence and Implications*. London: Health Education Authority.

Bilton, H. (1999) *Outdoor Play in the Early Years. Management and Innovation*. London: David Fulton.

Birch, H.D. and Lefford, A. (1967) Visual differentiation, intersensory integration and voluntary motor control. *Monographs of the Society for Research in Child Development*, 32: 1–87.

Bjorkvold, J.-R. (1989) *The Muse Within – Creativity and Communication, Song and Play from Childhood Through Maturity*. New York: HarperCollins.

Black, K. and Haskins, D. (1996) Including all children in TOP PLAY and BT TOP SPORT. *Primary PE Focus*, Winter: 9–11.

Blair, S.N., Kohl, H.W. and Gordon, N.F. (1992) Physical activity and health: a life-style approach. *Medicine, Exercise, Nutrition and Health*, 1: 54–7.

Blakemore, C. (1990) *The Mind Machine*. London: BBC Books.

Blamires, M. (1999) Universal design for learning: re-establishing differentiation as part of the inclusion agenda! *Support for Learning*, 14(4): 158–63.

Borcham, C., Savage, J., Primrose, E. *et al.* (1992) Risk factor assessment in school-children: the Northern Ireland 'young hearts' project. *Journal of Sports Sciences*, Conference Communications, 10: 565.

Bower, T.G.R. (1976) *Development in Infancy*. San Francisco, CA: W.H. Freeman.

Brazelton, T.B. (1984) *Neonatal behavioural scales*. Philadelphia, PA: J.B. Lippincott.

Bruininks, R.H. (1978) *Bruininks-Oseretsky Test for Motor Proficiency*. Circle Pines, MN: American Guidance Service.

Bruner, J.S. (1983) *Child's Talk*. Oxford: Oxford University Press.

Carlson, K. and Cunningham, J.L. (1990) Effect of pencil diameter on the grapho-motor skill of preschoolers. *Early Childhood Research Quarterly*, 5(2): 279–93.

Carroll, R. (1994) *Assessment in Physical Education*. London: Falmer Press.

Central Statistical Office (1994) *Social Focus on Children*. London: HMSO.

Chinn, S. and Rona, R.R. (2001) Prevalence and trends in overweight and obesity in three cross-sectional studies of British children 1974–94. *British Medical Journal*, 322: 24–36.

Christina, R.W and Corcos, D.M. (1988) *Coaches Guide to Teaching Sports Skills*. Champaign, IL: Human Kinetics.

Clark, J.E. (1988) Development of voluntary motor skill, in E. Meisami and P.S. Timitas (eds) *Handbook of Human Growth and Developmental Biology*. Boca Raton, FL: CRC Press.

Clark, J.E. and Phillips, S.J. (1993) A longitudinal study of intralimb coordination in the first year of independent walking: a dynamical systems analysis. *Child Development*, 64(4): 1143–57.

Cohen, L.B., Bruce, V., Green, P. and Georgeson, M. (1996) *Visual Perceptions*. New York: Psychology Press.

Corbin, C., Pangrazi, R. and Welk, G. (1994) Toward an understanding of appropriate physical activity levels for youth. *Physical Activity and Fitness Research Digest*, 1(8): 1–8.

Coren, S., Porac, C. and Duncan, P. (1981) Lateral preference behaviours in preschool children and young adults. *Child Development*, 52: 4433–50.

Cratty, B.J. (1979) *Perceptual and Motor Development in Infants and Children*. Englewood Cliffs, NJ: Prentice-Hall.

Cratty, B.J. (1986) *Perceptual and Motor Development in Infants and Children*, 3rd edn. Englewood Cliffs, NJ: Prentice-Hall.

Cullen, J. (1993) Preschool children's use and perceptions of outdoor play areas. *Early Child Development and Care*, 89: 43–53.

Davies, A. (2000) Teaching dance, in R.P. Bailey and T.M. Macfadyen (eds) *Teaching Physical Education 5–11*. London: Continuum.

Dennison, P. and Dennison, G. (1989) *Brain Gym: Teacher's Edition*. Ventura, CA: Edu-Kinesthetics.

Department for Education and Employment (1999a) *Curriculum Guidance for the Foundation Stage*. London: QCA/DfEE.

Department for Education and Employment (1999b) *Early Learning Goals*. London: QCA/DfEE.

Department for Education and Employment (1999c) Physical Education. *The National Curriculum for England and Wales*. London: QCA/DfEE.

Department for Education and Science (1972) *Movement. Physical Education in the Primary Years*. London: HMSO.

Department for Education and Science (1978) *Special Educational Needs (Warnock Report)*. London: HMSO.

Department for Education and Science (1991) *Physical Education for Ages 5–16*. London: HMSO.

Department for Health (1995) *Health of the Nation: Obesity, Reversing the Increasing Problem of Obesity in England*. London: DoH.

Department of National Heritage (1995) *Sport: Raising the Game*. London: DNH.

De Vries, J.I.P., Visser, G. and Prechtl, G. (1982) The emergence of fetal behaviour in qualitative aspects. *Early Human Development*, 7: 301–22.

Dowling, M. (1992) *Education 3–5*. London: Paul Chapman.

DuRant, R.H., Baranowski, T., Johnson, M. and Thompson, W.O. (1994) The relationship among television watching, physical activity and body composition of young children. *Pediatrics*, 94: 449–55.

Espenschade, A.S. (1947) Development of motor coordination in boys and girls. *Research Quarterly*, 18: 30–44.

Evans, J. and Roberts, G.C. (1987) Physical competence and the development of children's peer relations. *Quest*, 39: 23–35.

Field, T.M. (1990) *Infancy*. Cambridge, MA: Harvard University Press.

Freedman, D.S., Khan, L.K., Dietz, W.H., Srinivasan, S.R. and Berenson, G.S. (2001) Relationship of childhood obesity to coronary heart disease risk factors in adulthood: the Bogalusa heart study. *Pediatrics*, 108: 712–18.

Gabbard, C.P. (1992) *Lifelong Motor Development*. Dubuque, IA: WCB McGraw-Hill.

Gallahue, D.L. (1982) *Understanding Motor Development in Children*. New York: Wiley.

Gallahue, D.L. (1989) *Understanding Motor Development*, 2nd edn. Indianapolis, IN: Benchmark Press.

Gallahue, D.L. (1993) *Developmental Physical Education for Today's Children*. Dubuque, IA: Brown and Benchmark.

Gallahue, D.L. and Ozmun, J.C. (1995) *Understanding Motor Development*. Dubuque, IA: WCB Brown and Benchmark Publishers.

Gesell, A. (1939) *Infancy and Human Growth*. New York: Macmillan.

Graham, G., Holt-Hale, S. and Parker, M. (1993) *Children Moving. A Reflective Approach to Teaching Physical Education*. London: Mayfield Publishing Company.

Gross J. (1996) *Special Educational Needs in the Primary School*, 2nd edn. Milton Keynes: Open University Press.

Guthrie, E.R. (1952) *The Psychology of Learning*. New York: Harper and Row.

Hannaford, C. (1995) *Smart Moves. Why Learning is Not all in your Head.* Arlington, VI: Great Ocean Publishers.

Hardman, K. and Marshall, J.J. (2001) *Worldwide Survey on the State and Status of Physical Education in Schools.* Berlin: ICSSPE.

Hardy, C.A. (2000) Teaching swimming, in R.P. Bailey and T.M. Macfadyen (eds) *Teaching Physical Education 5–11.* London: Continuum.

Harris, J. and Elbourn, J. (1997) *Teaching Health-Related Exercise at Key Stage 1 and 2.* Champaign, IL: Human Kinetics.

Haywood, K.M. (1993) *Life Span Motor Development.* Champaign, IL: Human Kinetics.

Heald, C. (1998) *Physical Development.* London: Scholastic.

Health Education Authority (1997) *Young People and Physical Activity – A Literature Review.* London: HEA.

Heath, W., Smith, J., Gregory, C. *et al.* (1994) *Blueprints. Physical Education Key Stage 1.* Cheltenham: Stanley Thornes.

Henniger, M.L. (1985) Preschool children's play behaviours in an indoor and out-door environment, in J.L. Frost and S. Sunderlin (eds) *When Children Play. Proceedings of the International Conference on Play and Play Environments.* Wheaton, MD: Association for Childhood Education International.

Hillman, M. (1993) One false move . . . an overview of the findings and issues they raise, in M. Hillman (ed.) *Children, Transport and the Quality of Life.* London: Policy Studies Institute.

Hobart, C. and Frankel, J. (1994) *A Practical Guide to Child Observation.* Cheltenham: Stanley Thornes.

Hofsten, C. and Ronnqvist, L. (1993) The structuring of neonatal arm movements. *Child Development,* 64(4): 1046–57.

Hofstetter, C.R., Hovell, M.E., Sallis, J.F. *et al.* (1995) Exposure to sports mass media and physical activity characteristics among ethnically diverse adolescents. *Medicine, Exercise, Nutrition and Health,* 4: 234–42.

Hopper, B., Grey, J. and Maude, T. (2000*) Teaching Physical Education in the Primary School.* London: Routledge Falmer.

Hurst, V. and Joseph, J. (1998) *Supporting Early Learning.* Buckingham: Open University Press.

Hutt, S., Tyler, S. and Hutt, C. (1989) *Play, Exploration and Learning: A Natural History of the Pre-school.* London: Routledge.

Jenkinson, J.C. (1997*) Mainstream or Special: Educating Students with Disabilities.* London: Routledge.

Jensen, E. (2000) *Learning with the Body in Mind.* San Diego, CA: The Brain Store.

Keogh, J. and Sugden, D. (1985) *Movement Skill Development.* New York: Macmillan.

Klahr, D. and MacWhinney, B. (1998) Information processing, in W. Damon (gen. ed.), D. Kuhn and R.S. Siegler (vol. eds) *Handbook of Child Psychology. 2, Cognition, perception and language.* New York: Wiley.

Klesges, R.C., Mallot, J.M., Boschee, P.F. and Weber, J.M. (1986) The effects of parental influence on children's food intake, physical activity, and relative weight. *International Journal of Eating Disorders,* 5: 335–46.

Korner, A.F., Zeanah, C.H., Linden, J. *et al.* (1985) The relation between neonatal and later activity and temperament. *Child Development*, 56: 38–42.

Kotulak, R. (1996) *Inside the Brain*. Kansas City, KS: Andrews and McMeel.

Knobloch, H. and Pasamanick, B. (eds) (1974) *Gesell and Amatruda's Developmental Diagnosis*. New York: Harper and Row.

Krogman, W.M. (1980) *Child Growth*. Ann Arbor, MI: University of Michigan Press.

Laban, R. (1947) *Effort*. London: MacDonald and Evans.

Lasenby, M. (1990) *The Early Years. A Curriculum for Young Children. Outdoor Play.* London: Harcourt Brace Jovanovich.

Lerner, R.M. (1985) Adolescent maturational changes and psychosocial development: A dynamic interactional perspective. *Journal of Youth and Adolescence*, 14: 355–72.

Logsdon, B. *et al.* (1984) *Physical Education for Children: A Focus on the Teaching Process*. Philadelphia, PA: Lea and Febiger.

Lowrey, G.H. (1986) *Growth and Development of Children*. Chicago, IL: Year Book Medical Publishers.

McClenaghan, B.A. and Gallahue, D.L. (1978) *Fundamental Movement: A Developmental and Remedial Approach*. Philadelphia, PA: W.B. Saunders.

Macfadyen, T.M. and Bailey, R.P. (2002) *Teaching Physical Education 11–18*. London: Continuum.

Macfadyen, T.M. and Osborne, M. (2000) Teaching games, in R.P. Bailey and T.M. Macfadyen (eds) *Teaching Physical Education 5–11*. London: Continuum.

McGill, H.C. (1984) Persistent problems in the pathogenesis of artherosclerosis. *Artherosclerosis*, 4: 443–51.

McLean, S.V. (1991) *The Human Encounter: Teachers and Children Living Together in Preschools*. London: Falmer Press.

Magill, R.A. (1993) *Motor Learning. Concepts and Applications*. Dubuque, IA: Brown and Benchmark.

Malina, R.M. (1996) Tracking of physical activity and physical fitness across the lifespan. *Research Quarterly for Exercise and Sport*, 67(3)(Suppl): S1–S10.

Malina, R.M. and Bouchard, C. (1991) *Growth, Maturation and Physical Activity*, Champaign, IL: Human Kinetics.

Manners, H.K. and Carroll, M.E. (1995) *A Framework for Physical Education in the Early Years*. London: Falmer Press.

Maude, P. (2001) *Physical Children, Active Teaching. Investigating Physical Literacy.* Buckingham: Open University Press.

Mittler, P. (2000) *Moving Towards Inclusive Education: Social Contexts*. London: David Fulton Publishers.

Moore, L.L., Lombardi, D.A., White, M.J. *et al.* (1991) Influence of parents' physical activity levels on activity levels of young children. *Journal of Pediatrics*, 118: 215–19.

Mosston, M. and Ashworth, S. (1986) *Teaching Physical Education*. Columbus, OH: Merrill.

Mutrie, N. and Parfitt, G. (1998) Physical activity and its link with mental, social and moral health in young people, in S. Biddle, J. Sallis and N. Cavill (eds) *Young and Active? Young People and Health-enhancing Physical Activity – Evidence and Implications*. London: Health Education Authority.

NAHT (1999) NAHT publishes the results of its survey of PE and sports in schools, press release, 4 March.

Nichols, B. (1990) *Moving and Learning. The Elementary School Physical Education Experience*. St Louis, MI: Times Mirror/Mosby College Publishing.

Ofsted (Office for Standards in Education) (1996) *Physical Education and Sport in Schools: A Survey of Good Practice*. London: HMSO.

Oliver M. (1996) *Understanding Disability: From Theory to Practice*. Basingstoke: Macmillan.

Parry, J. (1998) The justification for physical education, in K. Green and K. Hardman (eds) *Physical Education: a reader*. Aachen: Meyer and Meyer.

Parsons, L. and Fox, P. (1997) Sensory and cognitive functions. *International Review of Neurobiology*, 41: 225–71.

Pellegrini, A.D. and Smith, P.K. (1998) Physical activity play: the nature and function of a neglected aspect of play. *Child Development*, 69: 577–98.

Petlickoff, L. (1992) Youth sport participation and withdrawal: is it simply a matter of fun? *Pediatric Exercise Science*, 4(2): 5–10.

Piaget, J. (1952) *The Origins of Intelligence in Children*. New York: International Universities Press.

Prechtl, H.F.R. (1986) Prenatal motor development, in M.G. Wade and H.T.A. Whiting (eds) *Motor Development in Children: Aspects of Coordination and Control*. Dordrecht: Martinus Nijhoff.

Ratey, J. (2001) *A User's Guide to the Brain*. London: Little, Brown and Company.

Reynolds, T. (2000) Teaching gymnastics, in R.P. Bailey and T.M. Macfadyen (eds) *Teaching Physical Education 5–11*. London: Continuum.

Riddoch, C. (1998) Relationships between physical activity and physical health in young people, in S. Biddle, J. Sallis and N. Cavill (eds) *Young and Active? Young people and health-enhancing physical activity – evidence and implications*. London: HEA.

Rink, J. (1993) *Teaching Physical Education for Learning*, 2nd edn. St Louis, MI: Mosby.

Robson, S. (1996) The physical environment, in S. Robson, and S. Smedley (eds) *Education in Early Childhood*. London: David Fulton.

Ross, A.O. (1976) *Psychological Aspects of Learning Disabilities and Reading Disorders*. New York: McGraw Hill.

Rowland, T.W. (1985) Aerobic response to endurance training in prepubescent children: a critical analysis. *Medicine and Science in Sports and Exercise*, 17: 493–7.

Rowland, T.W. (1990) *Exercise and Children's Health*. Champaign, IL: Human Kinetics.

Rowland, T.W. (1998) The biological basis of physical activity. *Medicine and Science in Sports and Exercise*, 30: 392–9.

Sallis, J.F. (1993) Promoting healthful diet and physical activity, in S.G. Millstein,

A.C. Petersen and E.O. Nightingale (eds) *Promoting the Health of Adolescents.* New York: Oxford University Press.

Sallis, J.F. (1995) A behavioral perspective on children's physical activity, in L.W.Y. Cheung and J. Richmond (eds) *Child Health, Nutrition and Physical Activity.* Champaign, IL: Human Kinetics.

Sallis, J.F. and Owen, N. (1999) *Physical Activity and Behavioral Medicine.* Thousand Oaks, CA: Sage.

Satterly, D. (1989) *Assessment in Schools.* Oxford: Blackwell.

Scarr, S. and McCartney, K. (1983) How people make their own environments: a theory of genotype/environment effects. *Child Development*, 54: 424–35.

Schickedanz, J.A., Schickedanz, D.I., Hansen, K. and Forsyth, P.D. (1993) *Understanding Children.* London: Mayfield Publishing Company.

Schmidt, R.A. (1977) Schema theory: Implications for movement education. *Motor Skills: Theory Into Practice*, 2: 36–8.

Schmidt, R.A. (1988) *Motor Control and Learning.* Champaign, IL: Human Kinetics.

Scott, S., Harden, J., Jackson, S. and Backett-Milburn, K. (2000) The impact of risk and parental risk anxiety on the everyday worlds of children. *Children 5–16 Research Briefing (Economic and Social Research Council)*, No. 19.

Scraton, S. (1993) Equality, coeducation and physical education in the secondary school, in J. Evans (ed.) *Equality, Education and Physical Education.* London: Falmer Press.

Shaffer, D.R. (1999) *Development Psychology. Childhood and Adolescence.* Pacific Grove, CA: Brooks/Cole Publishing Company.

Sharp, B. (1992) *Acquiring Skill in Sport.* Burgess Hill: Sports Dynamics.

Sharp, C. (1991) The exercise physiology of children, in V. Grisogono (ed.) *Children and Sport – Fitness, Injuries and Diet.* London: John Murray.

Siegler, R.S. (1996) *Emerging Minds: The Process of Change in Children's Thinking.* New York: Oxford University Press.

Sleap, M. and Warburton, P. (1996) Physical activity levels of 5–11-year-old children in England: cumulative evidence from three direct observation studies. *International Journal of Sports Medicine*, 17: 248–53.

Spackman, L. (1998) Assessment and recording in physical education. *British Journal of Physical Education*, 29(4): 6–9.

Sports Council (1988) *Children's Exercise and Health Fact Sheet.* London: Sports Council.

Sports Council (1993) *Young People and Sport.* London: Sports Council.

Sutcliffe, M. (1993) *Physical Education Activities. Bright Ideas for Early Years.* Warwickshire: Scholastic Publications.

Svejda, M. and Schmidt, D. (1979) The role of self-produced locomotion on the onset of fear of heights on the visual cliff. Paper presented at the Society for Research in Child Development, San Francisco.

Talbot, M. (1999) The case for physical education. Paper presented at the World Summit on Physical Education, Berlin, November.

Tanner, J.M. (1978) *Fetus into Man: Physical Growth from Conception to Maturity.* Cambridge, MA: Harvard University Press.

Thelen, E. (1979) Rhythmical stereotypes in normal human infants. *Animal Behaviour*, 27: 699–715.

Thelen, E. (1980) Determinants of amount of stereotyped behaviour in normal human infants. *Ethology and Sociobiology*, 1: 141–50.

Thelen, E. (1995) Motor development: a new synthesis. *American Psychologist*, 50: 79–95.

Thelen, E. and Ulrich, B.D. (1991) Hidden skills: A dynamic analysis of treadmill stepping during the first year. *Monographs of the Society for Research in Child Development*, 58(223).

Thelen, E., Corbetta, D., Kamm, K. *et al.* (1993) The transition to reaching: mapping intention and intrinsic dynamics. *Child Development*, 64: 1058–98.

Thelen, E., Ulrich, B.D. and Jensen, J.L. (1989) The developmental origins of locomotion, in M.H. Woollacott and A. Shumway-Cook (eds) *Development of Posture and Gait across the Life Span*. Columbia, SC: University of South Carolina Press.

Thomas, J.R. (1980) Acquisition of motor skills: information processing differences between children and adults. *Research Quarterly for Exercise and Sport*, 56(223): 158–73.

Thomas, J.R., Lee, A.M. and Thomas, K.T. (1988) *Physical Education for Children. Concepts into Practice*. Champaign, IL: Human Kinetics.

Ulrich, B.D. and Ulrich, D.A. (1985) The role of balancing in performance of fundamental motor skills in 3-, 4-, and 5-year old children, in J.E. Clark and J.H. Humphrey (eds) *Motor Development: Current Selected Research*. Princeton, NJ: Princeton Book Company.

Ulrich, D.A. (1985) *Test of Gross Motor Development*. Austin, TX: Pro-Ed.

UNESCO (1994) *The Salamanca Statement and Framework for Action*. Paris: UNESCO.

US Department of Health and Human Services (1996) *Physical Activity and Health: A Report of the Surgeon General*. Atlanta, GA: Centers for Disease Control.

Wein, B. (1988) Tiny Dancers. *Omni*: 122.

Werner, P. and Burton, E. (1979) *Learning Through Movement*. New York: Mosley.

Wetton, P. (1988) *Physical Education in the Nursery and Infant School*. London: Croom Helm.

Whitaker, R.C., Pepe, M.S., Wright, J.A., Seidel, K.D. and Dietz, W.H. (1998) Early adiposity rebound and the risk of adult obesity. *Pediatrics*, 101: 5–15.

Whitehead, M. (2000) The concept of physical literacy. Paper presented to the HEI Conference, 'Meeting Standards and Achieving Excellence. Teaching PE in the 21st Century'. Liverpool John Moores University, 11 June.

Wickens, C.D. (1974) Temporal limits of human information processing: a developmental study. *Psychological Bulletin*, 81: 739–55.

Wickstrom, R.L. (1983) *Fundamental Motor Patterns*. Philadelphia, PA: Lea and Febiger.

Williams, A. (1989) The place of physical education in primary education, in A. Williams (ed.) *Issues in Physical Education for the Primary Years*. London: Falmer.

Williams, H.G. (1983) *Perceptual and Motor Development*. Englewood Cliffs, NJ: Prentice-Hall.

Wold, B. and Hendry, L. (1998) Social and environmental factors associated with physical activity in young people, in S. Biddle, J. Sallis and N. Cavill (eds), *Young and Active? Young People and Health-enhancing Physical Activity – Evidence and Implications*. London: HEA.

Wright, H. and Sugden, D. (1999) *Physical Education for All.* London: David Fulton.

Wuest, D. and Bucher, C. (1995) *Foundations of Physical Education in Sport.* St Louis, MI: Mosby.

Index

PHYSICAL CHILDREN, ACTIVE TEACHING
INVESTIGATING PHYSICAL LITERACY

Patricia Maude

- How can children achieve their entitlement to gain physical literacy and to become physically educated?
- How can parents and teachers ensure that children's movement development and movement education are of the highest quality?
- What are the most appropriate contexts for facilitating children's physicality?

The book describes children's physical and movement development and analyses progression in motor skills from elementary to mature stages, from infancy through to the end of the primary school years.

Language development stemming from motor development and the contribution of language as a tool in the achievement of movement competence is discussed, as is the contribution of movement to children's play and creative activity.

The author addresses children's entitlement to become physically educated, both through the raising of standards in the physical education curriculum and through the heightening of expectations in children's knowledge, understanding, participation and performance in physical activity and the development of a healthy and active lifestyle.

Contents
Introduction – Physical motor development – Play – Language, creativity and physical literacy – Movement observation and assessment – Becoming physically educated – Physical literacy, active learning and active teaching – Conclusion – Bibliography – Index.

160pp   0 335 20572 0 (Paperback)   0 335 20573 9 (Hardback)